ANTHONY MUNDAY
THE ENGLISH ROMAYNE
LYFE.   1582

ELIZABETHAN AND JACOBEAN QUARTOS

ELIZABETHAN AND JACOBEAN QUARTOS
EDITED BY G. B. HARRISON

ANTHONY MUNDAY

THE ENGLISH ROMAYNE LYFE

1582

BARNES & NOBLE, Inc.
New York, New York

This edition published in 1966
by Barnes & Noble, Inc.
is reproduced from the series
BODLEY HEAD QUARTOS
published by
John Lane The Bodley Head Ltd., London
between 1922 and 1926

*N*ote

THE ORIGINAL of this text is in the British Museum (C. 25. c. 16).

The end of each page of the text is marked with / and the number of the page. In the original, only the pages of the text are numbered, the pagination of the preliminary matter being shown by the signatures.

The ornamental initial letters used in this reprint are facsimiles of those in the original text.

A list of the misprints which have been corrected will be found on page 106.

G. B. H.

Printed in the United States of America

INTRODUCTION

ANTHONY MUNDAY, one of the most prolific and versatile of Elizabethan writers, was born in London in 1553. In 1576 he was apprenticed to John Allde, the Stationer. Two years later he broke his indentures and went abroad with 'one Thomas Nowell.' Soon after leaving Boulogne, they were robbed of all their possessions, but they managed to reach Amiens, where they were looked after by an old English priest named Woodward, who sent them on to Dr. Allen at Rheims. Thence they set out for Rome to join the English College. After some months at Rome, Munday was sent back to England. He had evidently made himself well liked, and was trusted with messages and pictures, hallowed by the Pope, to be delivered to the Catholics in England. After his return (1578-9) he seems to have tried his hand at poetry and ballad-writing.

Two years later the authorities were much alarmed by the activities of Edmund Campion and other Jesuit missionaries who had come over from Rome in disguise. Munday was now able to turn his Roman experiences to profitable account. As he had met many of the principal Jesuits at the English College, he was naturally a most valuable spy, and was taken on the staff of Richard Topcliffe, the notorious anti-recusant agent, as informer and pamphleteer. Topcliffe was a very efficient detective, and before long Campion and his fellows were arrested and brought to trial, Munday being a most important witness for the Crown.

Before a London jury the accused could have but small hope of escape. They were condemned, as Munday notes in his *Discouerie of Edmund Campion*—

> To be drawne on Hurdles to the place of execution, where they should be hanged tyll they were halfe dead, then to be cutte downe, their priuie members to be cutte off, and theyr entrayles taken foorth, and to be burned in the fire before theyr eyes: then their heads to be cut off, their bodies parted into foure quarters, to be disposed at her Maiesties pleasure, and the Lord God to receiue theyr soules to his mercie.
>
> (Sig. F4^v)

However, on this occasion, the Queen's mercy was such that this 'beastly, shameless transformation' was not carried out until the accused were quite dead. Munday himself attended all the executions to write up a stop-press account: *A breefe and true reporte*

INTRODUCTION vii

of the Execution of certaine Traytours at Tiborne, the xxviii, and xxx dayes of Maye, 1582.

On the scaffold, one of the condemned priests, Fr. Luke Kirbie, vehemently protested his innocence and declared that not even Munday knew anything against him. Thereupon the Sheriff called Munday from the crowd, and a most unseemly wrangle ensued. After which Kirbie began (Munday notes)—

'to talke of my being at *Roome*, what freendshippe he had shewed vnto mee, and had done the lyke vnto a number of English men, whome he well knew, not to be of that Religion, bothe out of his owne purse, as also be freending them to some of the Popes Chamber, he made conueyaunce for them thence, some tyme going fortie miles with them: when (quoth he) had my dealings beene knowne, I should hardlie haue beene well thought off.'

(Sig. C1^v)

As Munday makes no comment, these statements are probably true.

The official minister then joined in and tried to make Kirbie acknowledge his guilt. This led on to another argument on the question of the Pope's supremacy. But the crowd were now growing impatient, and so Kirbie was turned off.

Munday had no shame in the matter, although he admits that he had fared badly under cross-examination by the accused. It was perhaps due to this fact that he describes the sufferings of Fr. Campion with a savage exultation which makes the most nauseous reading.

Naturally enough there were many who looked on Munday as a contemptible and discredited witness. Some indeed doubted whether he had ever been to Rome at all. To answer these charges, he wrote the *English Romayne Life*, in which he gives a most vivid description of his adventures, his life in the English Seminary, and the various festivals, antiquities, and churches which he saw.

Munday, of course, ascribes the best of motives to himself. He claims to have kept his faith pure throughout, and all the time to have been in his country's service. But his word is very unreliable. On his own showing, he was a glib and facile liar who served himself well on all occasions. More probably, like many other disappointed 'scholars,'[1] he went to Rheims and Rome to see what he could get out of it. However, he had a strong

---

[1] See the closing lines of the First Part of *The Returne from Parnassus*:

> To Rome or Rheims I'le hye, led on by fate,
> Where I will end my dayes or mend my state.

sense of humour, and must thoroughly have enjoyed recording some of the unkind things said about Great Persons at home.[1]

After 1584, Munday returned to literature and wrote plays, ballads, city pageants, pamphlets, romances, and translations, and, of course, he quarrelled with Ben Jonson. To his contemporaries, he was probably most famous as a ballad writer, though not many of his compositions can now be identified. He is perhaps the 'fat, filthy ballet-maker' mentioned by Kemp in his *Nine Daies Wonder*.[2]

In later years he became the friend of John Stow, the Antiquary, and after his death continued Stow's work, bringing out a new edition of the *Survey* in 1618.

Munday lived to a very respectable old age and survived all his more famous literary contemporaries. He was buried in the church of St. Andrew, Coleman Street, where a monument was put up to his memory. The tomb was destroyed in the Great Fire, but, according to the 1633 edition of the *Survey*,[3] the inscription ran:

---

[1] See page 21.

[2] Vol. IV in the *Quartos*, page 31.

[3] Page 869.

To the memory
Of that ancient Servant to the City, with
his Pen, in divers imployments, especially the *Survay of London*,
Master *Anthony Munday*,
Citizen and Draper
of *London*.

He that hath many an ancient Tombstone read,
(In labour seeming, more among the *dead*
To live, than with the *living*) that survaid
Obstruse Antiquities, and ore them laid
Such vive and beauteous colours with his Pen,
That (spite of time) those old are new agen,
Vnder this Marble lies inter'd: His Tombe,
Clayming (as worthily it may) this roome,
Among those many monuments his Quill
Has so reviv'd, helping now to fill
A place (with those) in his *Survay*: in which
He has a monument, more faire, more rich,
Than polisht Stones could make him, wher he lies
Though dead, still living, and in That, nere dyes.

Obiit Anno Ætatis suæ 80. *Domini* 1633.
Augusti 10.

G. B. HARRISON.

King's College,
University of London.

THE ENGLISH
Romayne Lyfe.

Discouering:

The liues of the Englishmen at *Roome*: the orders of the English Seminarie: *the diſſention betweene the Engliſhmen and the VVelshmen: the baniſhing of the Engliſhmen out of Roome: the Popes ſending for them againe: a reporte of many of the paltrie Reliques in Roome: their Vautes vnder the grounde: their holy Pilgrimages: and a number other matters, worthy to be read and regarded of euery one.*

(∵)

There vnto is added, the cruell tiranny, vſed on an Engliſh man at Roome, his Chriſtian ſuffering, and notable Martirdome, for the Goſpell of Ieſus Chriſte, in Anno. 1581. VVritten by A. M. ſometime the Popes Scholler in the Seminarie among them.

Honos alit Artes.

Seene and allovved.

✤Imprinted at London, by *Iohn Charle-woode, for Nicholas Ling: dwelling in Paules Church-yarde, at the ſigne of the Maremaide.*
Anno. 1582.

To the right Honorable Sir Thomas Bromley, Knight, Lord Chaunceller of Englande: *William, Lorde Burleigh and Lord Treasorer: Robert,* Earle of Leicester, with all the rest of her Maiesties most Honourable priuie Councell. *A. M.* wisheth a happy race in continuall honour, and the fulnesse of Gods blessing in the day of ioy.

His Booke (right Honorable) as I haue beene care full to note downe nothing in it, that myghte impeach mee, either with error or vntrueth, mallice or affection to any, but euen haue ordered the same, according to certeintie and knowledge: so when I had fully finished it, and doone the vttermost of my endeuoure therein, I considered with my selfe, I was to present|

[A2

The Epistle

the same, to such personages of Honor, wisèdome, and grauitie, as, did mallice rule me, they coulde quickly espie it, or affecting my selfe to any, they woulde soone discerne it: then would Honour reprooue me for the one, & their noble nature reprehende me in the other.

To discharge my selfe of bothe these, and purchase the fauoure wherewith your Honors are continually adorned: I directed my compasse by trueth, perswading my selfe, that albeit in some, Veritas odium parit : *yet in your Honours,* Magna est veritas et pręualet.

Fewe woordes suffiseth your wisedomes, and circumstaũce without substaunce, may incurre disliking: accordinge as when J presented your Honours with my booke, called the Dis-|

[A2ᵛ

Dedicatorie.

couerie of Campion, *I promised, so now in my* English Romaine life, *I haue performed: thinking my selfe in as safe securitie, vnder your Honourable fauor, as* Vlisses *supposed himselfe vnder the buckler of* Aiax.

Your Honors euer in dutie,
Anthonie Munday./ [A3

To the courteous and freend-
lie Reader.

He thing long promised (gentle Reader) is now perfourmed at last, and that which my aduersaries thought I would neuer set forth, to their disproofe and thy profit, I haue now published. Thou shalt find a number of matters comprehended within this small volume: some, that will irritate the minde of anie good subiect, and therfore to be read with regard: others, importing the whole course of our Englishmens liues in *Roome*, with the od conceits, and craftie iuglings of the Pope, (whereto our Englishmen are likewise conformable) they are in such true & certaine order set downe, as if thou were there thy selfe to behold them. I will not vse manie words, now thou hast it, read aduisedlie, condemne not rashlie, and if thou thinkest mee woorthie anie thanks for my paines, then freendlie bestowe it on me.

Thine in courtesie,
    Anthonie Munday. / [A4

¶ The English Romaine lyfe,

Discoursing the liues of such Englishe men, as by secret escape, leaue their owne Countrey, to liue in *Roome*, vnder the seruile yoke of the *Popes* gouernment. Also after what manner they spend their time there, practising, and daylie looking for, the ouerthrowe and ruine of their Princesse and Countrey.

First, howe the Authour left his natiue Countrey of England, betaking himselfe to trauell, and what happened in his iourney toward Roome.

Chap. 1.

Ecause a number haue been desirous, to vnderstand the successe of my iourney to *Roome*, and a nūber beside are doubtfull, whether I haue beene there or no, albeit the proofes thereof, sufficiently are extant to be seene: as well to content the one, as remoue the doubt of the other, I will (God ayding mee) heere set downe such a certaintie thereof, that if it happen not to please bothe, yet, if they will, it may profite bothe.

THE ENGLISHE

When as desire to see straunge Countreies, as also affection to learne the languages, had perswaded me to leaue my natiue Countrey, and not any other intent or cause, God is my record: I committed the small wealth I had, into my purse, a Trauelers weede on my backe, / the whole state and condition of [1 my iourney to Gods appointment, and beeing accompanied with one *Thomas Nowell*, crossed the Seas from *England* to *Bulloine* in *Fraunce*. From thence we trauelled to *Amiens*, in no small daunger, standing to the mercie of dispoyling Soldiers, who went robbing and killing thorowe the Countrey, the Campe beeing by occasion broken vp at that tyme. Little they left vs, and lesse would haue done, by the value of our liues, had not a better bootie come then we were at that time: the Soldiers preparing towards them, whome they sawe better prouided for their necessitie: offered vs the leysure to escape, which we refused not, beeing left bare enough, bothe of coyne and cloathes. But as then we stoode not to accoumpt on our losse, it suffised vs that we had our liues: whereof beeing not a little glad, we set the better legge before, least they should come backe againe, and robbe vs of them too.

This our misfortune vrged vs to remembraunce, of our former quiet beeing in

[marginal note: The Camp broken vp, the soldiers met with vs, & robbed vs, & hardly did we escape with our liues.]

England, carefullie tendered by our Parents, and loouingly esteemed among our freends, all which we vndutifullie regarding, rewarded vs with the rod of our owne negligence: beeing as then fearefull of all company on the way, such cruell and heauy spectacles was still before our eyes, but yet this did somewhat comfort vs, we had nothing woorth the taking from vs, but our liues, which we had good hope to saue, either by their pittie, or our owne humble perswasion.

Many men robbed and slaine by the Soldiers, which made vs trauell in no small feare.

When we were come to *Amiens*, we were giuen to vnderstande, that there was an olde Englishe Preest in the Towne, whose name was Maister *Woodward*: of whome we perswaded our selues, for Countrey sake, to finde some courtesie, in hope whereof, we enquired for his lodging, and at last found him. After such salutations as passe betweene Countreymen at their meeting, I began to tell him, howe we had left our Countrey, for the / earnest desire we had to see forraine [2 Dominions, howe we had beene spoyled by the way, of all that we had, and that we hoped for some freendship at his handes, which if God vouchsafed vs safe returne, should not be cast out of remembraunce.

The Preest of whome I haue made mencion in my Discouerie of Campion.

Alas my freendes (quoth he) I am your Countreyman I will not denie, but not such a one as you take me for. I am a poore Preest, and heere I liue for my conscience sake, whereas, were thinges according as they should be, it were better for me to be at home in mine owne Countrey. And yet trust me, I pittie to see any of my Countreymen lacke, though I am not able any way to releeue them: there be daylie that commeth this way, to whome, according to my hability, I am liberall, but they be such, as you are not, they come not for pleasure but for profite, they come not to see euerie idle toye, and to learne a little language, but to learne how to saue bothe their owne and their freendes soules, and such I would you were, then I could say that to you, which (as you be) I may not.

Trust me Sir (quoth I) I hope we haue learned to saue our soules already, or else you might esteeme vs in a verie bad case. If you haue (quoth he) it is the better for you, but I feare me one day, they that teach you to saue your soules after that manner, will pay for it deerelie, and you with them for company.

With these wordes, he began to wexe somewhat melancholie, which I perceiuing, and remembring that our necessitie, stoode not in case to pleade pointes of controuersie: rather sought to please him in hope of some lyberalitie, then to contend with him (we beeing vnable) and so fall into farder daunger.

ROMAINE LYFE

Whervpon I desired him, not to be offended at any thing we had sayde, for we would gladlie learne any thing that might benefite vs, and beside, would follow his counsaile in any reasonable cause. / Then he began to be [3 somewhat more gentlie disposed, saying, he could not greatlie blame vs, if we were obstinate in our opinion, comming from such a young Hell as we dyd, but he had good hope, that ere long it would be harrowed.

Then he willed vs to walke with him, and he would bring vs where we should lodge that night, at his charges: all the way rehearsing vnto vs, how beneficiall the Pope was to our Countreymen, and howe highlie we might pleasure our selues, our freendes and Countrey, if we would followe his councell. Beside, such horrible and vnnaturall speeches, he vsed against her Maiestie, her honourable Councell, and other persons that he named: as the verie remembraunce maketh me blushe, and my heart to bleede. To all which we gaue him the hearing, but God knowes, on my parte, with what anguishe of minde: for I would haue perswaded my selfe, that duety should haue with-helde the Subiect from reuiling his Princesse, and nature from slaundering his owne Countrey: but it suffiseth, where grace is absent, good qualities can neuer be present.

The Preeste vsed many circumstaunces, of the Popes lyberality to our Countreymen: as also what Treasons was toward her Maiestie and the Realme.

When wee were come to our Lodging, he talked with our Hostesse, what she should prouide for us, and afterward taking his leaue, tolde vs he woulde haue more talke with vs in the morning: in the meane time, we should thinke on that, which he had opened to vs, and resolue our selues on a certayne determination, for he meant vs more good then we were beware off. He beeing departed, we fell to such simple cheere as was prepared for vs, which was simple in deed, scant sufficient to the good stomackes we had to our victualles: but because we had soone done, we went the sooner to bed, sparing as much time as we could, in remembraunce of the Preestes woordes, tyll the wearinesse of our iourney, compelled vs to take our rest.

A little suffiseth hunger, where necessitie is mistresse of the feast.

In the morning, the Preest sent a poore fellow, whom / he kept to make his bed, [4 and run about on his errandes, to our lodging, that we should come vnto his Maister presently, because he had occasion to goe into the Town, and his returne was vncertaine, therefore he would speake with vs before he went. Vpon these so hasty summons, we addressed our selues towards him, finding him in his Chamber, reading vpon his Portesse, to him we gaue thankes for his courtesie, promising to requite it if he came where we might doo it. In breefe, among

ROMAINE LYFE 7

great circumstaunce of talke, wherein he manifested the treason toward *England*: he behaued him selfe in speeches to vs, according as I haue already declared in my *Discouerie of Campion*, where you may perceyue the Popes determination, & our Englishmẽs vnnatural consent, to be Traitors to their own Princesse, to shorten her life, & ouerthrow their natiue Coũtrey, where they were borne.

There you maye reade his woorde, at large set downe.

When he had mightily besieged vs with a multitude, as well threatninges as perswasions, to conforme our selues vnder that obedience: as well to auoide perill that might otherwise happen, as also to gayne somewhat towarde our releefe, we promised him to doo as he would haue vs, & to goe whether he would appoint vs. Whervpon he presentlie wrote two Letters to Doctor *Allen* at *Rheimes*, one of them cõcerned our preferment there, howe we should be entertayned into the Englishe Seminarie, and take the orders of Preesthood, because we might doo good in our Countrey an other day. The other Letter was of such newes, as he heard out of *England*, howe matters went forewarde to their purpose, and beside, other thinges which I am not to speake of heere, because they are not to be read of euerie one.

These Letters finished, and sealed vp with singing Cake, he delyuered vnto vs, saying:

THE ENGLISHE

I thanke God that I am ordayned the man, bothe to saue your Soules, and a number of your freendes heere in *England*, whome I [5 could wishe heere present with you, for that I pittie their estate, as well that they are in, as that which is wurse, and I feare mee will fall on them shortlie.

I put vp the Letters, and gaue him to vnderstande, that we could hardlie trauell from thence to *Rheimes*, hauing nothing wherwithall we might beare our charges. Trust me (quoth he) & I haue done as much for you as I am able, for I haue nothing heere but to serue mine owne necessitie. Then we offered to sell our Cloakes, which the Soldiers against their willes had left vs. In deede (quoth he) to trauell in your Cloakes will doo nothing but hinder you, I will send my man to a freend of mine (as much to saye, as his Chest) to see what money he can gette for them.

<small>When we offered to sel our Clokes: he could find money to buie them.</small>

The fellowe tooke our Cloakes, after his Maister had whispered him in the eare, and went downe the staires, returning quicklie with two French Crownes, which the Preest deliuered to vs, with fowre or fiue French *Souses* out of his owne Purse, so, willing vs to doo his commendations to Doctor *Allen*, and to labour earnestlie in that we went about: Maister *Woodward* and we parted, he into the Towne, and we on our iourney.

<small>Great lyberalitie.</small>

ROMAINE LYFE

When we were about three or fowre myles from *Amiens*, we sate downe on the side of a hyll, recounting what the Preest had sayde to vs, as also the cause why he sent vs to *Rheimes*: the remembraunce of the true and vndoubted Religion, vsed in our owne Countrey, and wherein we were trayned vp, was of force sufficient to perswade vs from yeelding to that, which we iudged rather to be a mummerie, and derision of the true Doctrine, then otherwise: So that (notwithstanding many matters my companion alleadged vnto me, what daunger we might come vnto, if we went not to deliuer the Letters, as also the harde penurie we should finde in trauell, beeing destitute of money, apparell, and all / other needeful thinges) [6 by the onelie appointment of God, who no doubt put it in my minde at that tyme, I willed him to followe me, and come woe, want, miserie, or any other calamitie, I would neuer leaue him to the death. But if any exercise might get it, any paines compasse it, or the extreme shifte of begging attayne it: I would doo all my selfe, whereby to maintaine vs, onelie that he would but beare me company, for I would trie all meanes that might be, ere I woulde forsake my Faith.

This to be true, I am sure and certayne him selfe will not denie, who seeing my

[6 This to be true, albeit he nowe be my vtter enimie, I am sure he will not denie.

earnest intreatie, and the promises I made to the vttermost of my power: agreed to goe with me, and so we left the way to *Rheimes*, and went on strayte to *Paris*.

In *Paris* we mette with a French man, who coulde speake a little broken Englishe, and he conducted vs where my Lord the English Ambassador laie: to whome I gaue the Letters, and after certaine talke he vsed with vs, he bestowed his Honourable lyberalitie vppon vs, wishing vs to returne backe againe into *England*.

<small>It is a good help, to meet a freend in a straunge Countrey, when a mã is in some neede.</small>

Leauing my Lord, and walking into the Cittie, we mette certayne Englishe Gentlemen, some of them for the knowledge they had of me in *England*, shewed them selues verie courteous to me, bothe in money, lodging, and other necessaries. And through them we became acquainted with a number of Englishe men more, who lay in the Cittie, some in Colledges, and some at their owne houses: where vsing dailie company among them, sometime at dinner, and sometime at supper, we heard many girdes and nippes against our Countrey of *England*, her Maiesty very vnreuerently handled in woords, and certayne of her honourable Counsell, vnduetifullie tearmed.

Great talke they had, about Doctor *Saunders*, who / they sayde, eyther as then [⁷

ROMAINE LYFE

was, or shortlie would be, arriued in *Ireland*, howe he had an Armie of Spaniardes with him, and howe him selfe vnder the Popes Standarde, would giue such an attempt there, as soone after should make all *England* to quake, beside, there were certaine Englishe men gone to the Pope, for more ayde, if neede should be, at whose returne, certaine Noble men English men, then beeing in those partes, whose names I omitte for diuers causes, would prosecute the matter, with as much speede as might be.

The very same did the Preest at *Amiens* giue vs to vnderstand of, almost in euerie point agreeing with this: which made vs to doubt, because in euerie mans mouth, her Maiesty styl was aimed at, in such mañer as I trēble and shake to thinke on their woordes. All this tyme that we remained amongst them, diuerse of the Gentlemen and others (who were lyke factors for the Pope, as Maister *Woodward* at *Amiens*, Doctor *Bristowe* at *Doway*, and Doctor *Allen* at *Rheimes* were, to encrease his Seminaries with as many Englishe men as they might,) verie earnestlie perswaded vs to trauell to *Roome*, assuring vs, that we should be there entertained to our high contentment, beside, they would giue vs Letters for our better welcome thether.

Any subiect, that hath either feare of God, or loue to his prince would quake to heare their Trayterous deuises. The Deuil wanteth no instruments to helpe his cause.

We were soone entreated to take the

THE ENGLISHE

iourney on vs, because we thought, if we could goe to *Roome*, and returne safelie againe into *England*, we should accomplish a great matter, the place beeing so farre of, and the voyage so daungerous. Vppon our agreement to vndertake the trauell, we receyued of euerie one lyberallie toward the bearing of our charges, and Letters we had to Maister Doctor *Lewes* in *Roome*, the Archdeacõ of *Cambra*, and to Doctor *Morris*, then the Rector of the English Hospital or Colledge in *Roome*, that we might there be preferred among the English Students. /   [8

By their perswasions and liberalitie, they win a number daylie to them.

Taking our leaue of them, and yeelding them thankes for their greate courtesy, we iournied to *Lyons*, where in the house of one Maister *Deacon*, the wordes were spoken by *Henry Orton*, one of them condemned, and yet liuing in the Tower, which in my other booke I haue auouched. From thence wee went to *Millaine*, where in the Cardinall *Boromehos* Pallace, we found the lodging of a Welshman, named Doctor *Robert Griffin*, a man there had in a good accoũt, and Cõfessor to the aforesaid Cardinal. By him we were very courteouslye entertained, and sent to the house of an Englishe Prieste in the Cittie, named Maister *Harries*, who likewise bestowed on vs very gentle acceptaunce, as also three English Gentlemẽ, who lay in his house,

There are Englishmen almoste in euery Cittie by the waye.

ROMAINE LYFE

being very lately retourned frõ *Roome*: they likewise both in cost and courtesie, behaued them selues like Gentlemen vnto vs, during the time that we made our abode in *Millaine*.

Our comming to *Millayne* was on Christmas euen, and hauing lyen that night at an *Osteria* where Maister *Harryes* appoynted vs, on Christmas day we dyned with Doctor *Griffin*, where we had great cheere, and lyke welcome. In the dinner time, he moued many questions vnto vs, as concerning the estate of England, if we heard of any warres towardes and howe the Catholiques thriued in Englande: and at the laste (quoth he) haue you not seene three Gentlemen that lye at Maister *Harryes* his house? Yes that we haue (quoth I) to vs they seeme meruailous curteous, and offer vs such freendshippe as we haue neuer deserued. Oh (quoth he) if all things had fallen right to their expectation, they would haue beene iolly fellowes. I am sure you haue heard what credite Captaine *Sukelye* was in with the Pope, and howe he was appointed w^t his Armie, to inuade England: he being slayne in the battaile of the King of *Portugall*, thinges went not forwarde according as they should haue done. These three Gentlemen came foorth of the North partes of *England*, taking vpon them to goe forward with that, which *Stukely* had

[margin: The talke that Doctor Griffen had with vs, being at dinner with him.]

enterprised, which was, to haue the Popes Armie committed to theyr conduction, and so they would ouerrun *England* at their pleasure, then they would make Kings and Dukes and Earles, euery one that they thought well off. To helpe them forwarde in this matter, they purchased the Letters of Doctor *Saunders*, Doctor *Allen*, Doctor *Bristow*, and others, who thought very well of their intent, & therfore furthered thẽ in their Letters so much as they might, to Doctor *Lewes*, Doctor *Morris*, Doctor *Moorton*, and diuers other Doctors and Gentlemen at *Roome*, all of thẽ verye earnestly following ye sute hereof to ye Popes holines, informing him, how they had already wun such a nũber in *England*, to ioin with thẽ when ye matter came to passe, ye graunting thẽ his holines Army, they would presently ouerrun all *England*, and yeelde it wholly into his hand. But when the Pope had scanned on this hasty busines, well noting the simple and arrogant behauiour of the men, and their vnlikelihoode, of performing these thinges: euen accordinge as they deserued, they were denyed theyr request, & sent a way without any recompence. The Pope was not to truste to any such as they, he well knowes *England* is too strong yet, & till the people be secretely perswaded, as I doubt not but there is a good

An vnnaturall desire of men to seeke the ruine of theyr owne Country.

The secret seducing Preestes, win a number to ioyne in theyr trayterous intent.

The Pope seeketh to accomplish his desire, by

number, and more & more still shalbe, by yᵉ *the Sub-*
Preests are sent ouer dayly, and they must war *iect that*
within, while other holds thẽ play with out: till *must*
then *England* will not be conquered any way. *betray his*
owne
Country.

Other talke we had, not heere to be
rehearsed, but truly it would astonishe a heart
of *Adamant*, to heare the horrible Treasons
inuented againste her Maiestie and this
Realme, and so greedily followed by our
owne Countrye men. But some perhaps will
de-/ maunde howe wee behaued our selues [10
to come to the knowledge of such trayterous
intentions, iudging yᵗ they would rather keepe
thẽ secret, then reueale them to any: to
aunswer such as so doo question, thus it was.

When I was at *Paris*, the Gentlemen tooke *The*
me to be a Gentlemans Sonne heere in *meane,*
wherby
England, whom I refuse heere to name, but *they*
as it seemed, they were somewhat perswaded *made me*
of him: I perceiuing they tooke mee for his *ac-*
quainted
Sonne, called my selfe by his name, where *with al*
through I was the better esteemed, and *their*
beside, loued as I had beene he in deede. *deuises.*
When they vnderstoode my fellowes name
to be *Thomas Nowell*, they whispered among
themselues, and sayd vndoubtedly, he was
kin to Maister *Nowell* the Deane of Paules:
and if they wist certainly that he were so,
they woulde vse him in such gentle order, as
they woulde keepe hym there, so that one

16   *THE ENGLISHE*

day he shoulde stande and preache against his Kinseman. This suppose, seruing so wel our necessitye, we were glad to vse: which made vs well thought on of all, and keeping company so familiarlye with them, we were made acquainted with a number more matters then may heere be expressed.

<small>The treason against England, was cõmon in euery Englishmãs mouth.</small>

While we were in *Millaine*, wee visited Maister Doctor *Parker*, who likewise told vs the same tale that Doctor *Griffin* had before rehearsed, beside, he tolde vs that Preestes were appointed from *Roome* & *Rheimes* for *Englande*, and that ere long they should be sent. Soone after we departed thence, to *Bologna*, *Florence*, *Scienna*, and so to *Roome*, wher how we were receiued the Chapter following shall amply vnfolde. Thus, as well to certifie the incredulous, as also to content those desirous howe I attained to *Roome*: I haue breeflye doone my good wyll to please bothe.

You haue hearde heerein, howe at sundrye places, and by seuerall speeches, there was a generall agreement of Treason, expected and daylye looked for, / to the harme of our [11 gracious Soueraigne, and hurte of her whole Realme. All these matters wee heard before we came to *Roome*, from whence the treason shoulde cheefely proceede: we seeing such deuillish deuises to be talked on by the way, we might well iudge *Roome* to be Hell it selfe, in that all thinges should goe forwarde, as it was there determined. You are not altogether ignoraunt of their intentes at *Roome*, for that my other booke hath truely reueled some of their traiterous and disloyall practises: and such as modestie will suffer me to vtter, and you to reade, you shall here finde faithfullye discoursed.

¶ *The Author beeing come to Rome, after what manner he was receiued into the Englishe Seminarie. The emulation & dissension, between the VVelshmen and the English men in the Colledge, their banishment out of Roome, & the Popes sending for thē againe, as you shall reade heareafter.*

Chap. 2.

Ur entraunce into *Roome*, was vppon *Candlemas* euen, when as it drew somewhat towardes nighte: for which cause, we refused as then to goe to the English Colledge, taking vp our Lodging in an *Osteria* somewhat within the Cittie, and determining to visit the Englishe house on the next morning. On the morrowe by enquiring, we founde the Englishe Colledge, where after we were once entered, wee had a number about vs quicklye, to knowe what newes in / England, and how all matters [12 went there. Not long had we stoode talking with them, but one entred the Colledge, with a great many of wax Candles in hys hande: who gaue them to vnderstande, that the Pope had sent to euery Scholler in the Colledge a Candle, which that day at high Masse he had hallowed, for it was *Candlemas* day. They receiuing thẽ with great account, both of the Popes fauoure, as also the holines they credited to consist in the Candles, went euery one to lay them vp in their Chambers: in the meane time Maister Doctor *Morris* the Rector of the house came to vs, to whom we deliuered the Letter sent to him on our behalfe from *Paris*, which when he had read, he said we were welcõe, allowing vs yᵉ eight dayes entertainment in the Hospitall, which by the Pope was graunted to such Englishmen as came thether. Then hee brought vs to Doctor *Lewes*, the Archdeacon of *Cambra*, to whom we deliuered his letter likewise, and with him we stayed dinner, ignorant whither he were an Englishman or no, for that he gaue vs our entertainment in Latine, demaunded a number of questions of vs in

Sidenote: A present of holy Candle brought from the Pope to the English Students.

ROMAINE LYFE

Latine, and beside, dined with vs in Latine: whereat we meruailed, till after dinner, he bad vs walke to the Colledge againe with Doctor *Morris*, in English. We were no sooner come to the Colledge, but the Schollers, who had already dined, and were walking together in the Court, came about vs, euerye one demaunding so many questions, that we knewe not which to aunswer first: at last, one of them tooke my fellow aside, and one of the Priestes lykewise desired to talke with me, because he sayd he knew my Father well enough, vsing the name that I did, so, he and I sitting together in the Garden, among other talke he asked of me, wherefore I came to *Rome*? Truste me Sir (quoth I) onely for the desire I had to see it, that when I came home againe, I might say, once in my life / I [13 haue beene at *Roome*. Then I perceiue (quoth he) you come more vpon pleasure then any deuotion, more desirous to see the Cittie, then to learne the vertues conteined in it: in sooth I see, you remaine in the same wildnes you did, when I lay at your Fathers house, but I doo not doubt now we haue you heere, to make you a stayed man ere you departe, that your Father may haue ioy of you, and all your freends receiue comfort by you. In deede Sir (quoth I) I haue alwayes addicted my mind to so many youthfull deuises, that I little

The talke one of the Priests had with me in the Garden.

THE ENGLISHE

<small>Mine owne tale, which so well as I could, I made to agree with the Preests discourse.</small>

regarded any religion, which my Parents seeing, and fearing I would neuer be bridled: sent me ouer to *Paris*, where I should remaine at my booke. But there I found Gentlemen of mine acquaintaunce, who wished me to trauell hither, whereto I quickly gaue my consent, beeing (as I haue told you) desirous to see a thing so famous. I thinke very well (quoth he) of your woordes, aswell for your Parents sake as also your owne. But this I will say vnto you, there ought none to come hither, the place being so holy, auncient, and famous, but onely such as with earnest endeuour, seeke and thirst after the Catholique faith: beeing heere taught and mainteined, according as Christ ordeyned it, the Apostles deliuered it, *Peter* himselfe planted it, and all the Fathers of the Church since, haue followed it. They must denounce that damnable heresie, crept in to the Church of *England*, that proude vsurping *Iezabell*, (meaning our dread & gracious Princesse) whom (quoth he) God reserueth to make her a notable spectacle to the whole world, for keeping ye good Queene of *Scots* frõ her lawfull rule: but I hope ere long, ye Dogs shall teare her flesh, & those y^t be her props & vpholders.

<small>Heere may you beholde, what vnreuerent speeches they can affoorde her Maiestie.</small>

<small>A paper of the names of</small>

Then drawing a paper out of his pocket, he sayd, I haue a Bead role of them heere, who little knowes what is prouiding for them, & I hope shall not know, till it fall vpon them. Then he read their names vnto me, which, that all may perceiue the villainous & trayterous mindes of our owne Countriemen: so many of them as I can call to memory, I will set down, euen in the same manner as he read thẽ. But first I must craue pardon of those honourable personages, to whome the words doo offer great abuse, and whom I vnfeynedlye reuerence and honour: that they would not admit any euill conceite against mee, but in the noble nature wherewith they are dayly adorned, I, beeing but the reporter, may be pardoned and not reprooued. First, (quoth he) heere is my Lord *Keeper*, the Bacon hogge, the Butchers sonne, the great guts, oh he woulde fry well with a Faggot, or his head would make a fayre showe vpon London bridge, where I hope shortly it shall stand. Next is eloquent Maister *Cecill*, Lorde *Treasorer*, you shall shortly see if he can saue his owne life with all ye wit he hath: had it not been for these two before named, *England* had gon to wracke long since. Then heere is the Earle of *Leicester*, the Queenes Ostler, & his brother *Ambrose Dudly*, a good fat whorson, to make Bacon of: with other words of my Lorde of *Leicester*, not here to be rehearsed. My Lord of *Bedforde*, he

[14 such noble men of her Maiesties Counsell, whom they meant to persecute, when their intent came to passe in England.

I desire thee gentle Reader, to vse some reuerence in reading these vndecent woords, because they are truly set downe, after the order as they were there spoken.

forsooth is yᵉ Queenes Coozin, we will see how finely his Coozin & he can hang together. Sir *Fraunces Walsinghã*, & Doctor *Wilson*, they be her Secretaries: for euery warrãt they haue suffered, to apprehend any of our Priestes, our freends or other, by that time they haue coũted their reckoning, they shall find they haue a deere payment. Sir *Christopher Hatton*, he pleased yᵉ Queene so wel, dauncing before her in a Maske, yᵗ since yᵗ time he hath risen to be one of yᵉ Counsell: with other words, which I referre for modestie. Sir *Fraunces Knowles*, and other of the Counsell whose names I well remember not: he gaue them many a heauy threatning. Then opening the paper farder, at the end therof was a great many of names, of Magistrates & other be- / longing to this Cittie, [15 among whome was Maister *Recorder*, Maister *Nowell* Deane of Paules, Maister *Foxe*, Maister *Crowlye*, & sundry other, whose names I cannot very well remember, and therefore am loth to set downe any thing, but that whereof I am certainly assured: but verye well I remember, there was no one named, but he had the order of his death appoynted, eyther by burning, hanging, or quartering, and such like.

It is not vnlike, but that this vnreuerent matter will offende some in the reading, that

<small>Euery one that was named in the paper, the manner and order of their death was appoynted.</small>

men of honour, and worshippe, and those of
credite and countenaunce, shoulde haue their
names published in print in suche sorte: I
haue had the iudgement of those, of worshippe and learning, on this behalfe, and
they haue sayde, how it is necessary, that theyr
owne wicked speeches should be set downe,
for an example to all men, howe they abuse
her Maiestie, her honourable Councell, and
learned and discreete Maiestrates, whereby
their trayterous dealings may be the better
discouered. And to them thus vndutifully
regarded, it can not seeme an offence, considering, that Christe vnto his chosen vessels
hath sayd. *You shall be mocked, scorned, and* Math. 5. 11.
*reuiled for my sake: but doo you reioyce and be
glad, for your rewarde is the greater in the
kingdome of Heauen, and you remaine blessed.*

Then putting vp his Paper agayne, he began after this manner. As I haue sayd before, so now I saye the same, such as come to this holy place, must faithfully bende his life and conuersation, to honour and reue- rence our prouident and holy Father the Pope, in all thinges, that shall like him to commaund, to holde and confesse him the vniuersall supreme heade of Christes church, & embrace his decrees, as the onely or- denance & will of God. For he is the person of God on earth, and he can not sinne, because *There are other heere, to whom the like charge hath beene, giuen to iustifie that I doo not re- port any vntrueth.*

the spirite of diuine grace / guideth him [16 continuallie: he hath aucthoritie ouer all Kinges and Princes, to erect and suppresse whome he pleaseth, and that shall *England* well knowe ere long, that he hath such power and aucthoritie. To honour and obey him, to be a true and faithfull member of his Church, and to liue and die in his cause, this ought to be the intent of all that commeth heere.

This long Tale, contayning a number of more circumstaunces than I can vnfolde: made me studie what aunswer I should make him, which after some pause, came foorth as thus. Credite me Sir, I am but a Nouesse in these matters, and therefore you might as well haue disputed with me, in the deepest Schoole-points that is, and I should haue censured bothe alike. Nay (quoth he) I thinke not your ignoraunce so great, albeit it seemeth great enough, though you haue beene looselie brought vp, yet you haue beene with me, bothe at Masse, and at Confession diuers times, at such time as I serued my Lady *B*.

<small>A number of places he tolde me heere in Englande, where preestes haue entertainement.</small>

Beside, there are a great many of Priestes in *England*, as in *Warwickshire*, at Maister *I. T.* in *Staffordshire*, at Maister *G.* of *C.* and at *S. T. F.* in the same shyre: all these be neere your Fathers, and not one of them but visiteth your Fathers house, three or fowre times euerie yeere, as they dyd when I was there (for there is no long tariaunce in one place for a Priest, but he must shifte styll, least he be taken,) and I am sure your Father would see you duelie confessed.

Nowe I was put to so harde a shifte, that I knewe not well what to say, I knewe none of these men he named, but one, and he in deede had a Priest, who after his long raunging about his Maister the Popes businesse heere in *England*, I thanke God, I haue caused to be stayed. Likewise, I knewe not the Gentleman, whome, bothe they at *Paris*, and he sayde, to be my Fa- / ther, neither [17 where he dwelt, nor what he was: which made me stand in feare to be disproowed, hauing auouched my selfe before to be his Sonne. Wherfore, referring my case to God, who had so prouided for me tyll that time, in his name I resolued my selfe on this aunswer, not knowing howe it might happen to speede.

It was only God, that framed my aunswers to agree with the Preests demaunds.

In deede Sir, I can not denie, but that I haue oftentimes heard Masse, as also beene at Confession, but my deuotion thereto hath beene slender, as you your selfe haue seene, knowing me to be so wilde, and, as it were, without gouernment: but when you departed from my Fathers, I taried there but a small time after you, for I obtayned leaue of my Father, to goe lye at London, at a Kinsemans house of his, because I would studie the

An excuse seruing very fit for my purpose, and lyked the Preest well enough.

French tongue, to haue some knowledge therein against I went ouer, for my Father tolde me long before, that I should goe to *Paris*, and studie there. When I was at London, I grewe in acquaintaunce with diuers Gentlemen, in whose company I frequented many delightfull pastimes: so that I could hardlie refraine them, when my Father sent for me, to the intent I should trauell to *Paris*.

Well (quoth he) and though you did goe to London so soone after I was gone, any of the Preestes that resorted to your Fathers, or he him selfe could haue certified you, of such places in London, where you might haue heard Masse, and beene Confest too, without suspect at all. For at Maister *S.* his house on the backside of *P.* you might diuers times haue heard Masse, and beene Cõfest there likewise: I lay there an indifferent while, and sayd Masse there, wherat diuers were present, also in the after noone, when they haue beene at the Play, in all that time I haue Confessed many.

Likewise, you might haue gone to the Marshalsea, and enquired for Maister *Pownd*, & you should sildom / haue missed, but haue [18] found a Preest there with him: for sometime vnder ye habites of Gentlemen, Seruing-men, or what apparell they imagine most conuenient for them, Preestes doo daylie resorte

A matter woorthy to be regarded.

Euerarde Ducket, was taken, going into the Marshalsea,

vnto him, where they confesse him, and giue him such halowed things as are sent him from *Roome*, as *Agnus Deis, Grana benedicta*, and other things: there, if you had made him priuie to your intent, he would haue appointed one that should haue done it for you. He likewise would haue bestowed on you some of those holie thinges, for he findeth such meanes, what with the Preests that come to him, and other, whome he hyreth or intreateth to cary a Letter abroade now and then for him: that those holie thinges are deliuered to their handes, who doo not a little reioyce in them. My selfe once, made *Norris* the Pursuiuant carie a Letter for me, to one of my Lady *B*. her Gentlewomen: and therin was two *Agnus Deis*, a hallowed Girdle, and aboue fortie or fiftie *Grana benedicta*, which maketh me to smile euerie time I thinke on it, that I could make him my man, when I durst not deliuer it my selfe.

to speake with the Papists he beeing a Preest: and beeing there taken, behaued him selfe in such trayterous manner, that he was executed at Tiborne, 1581.

Maister *Norris* beeing told this: offereth his life, if any such thing can be prooued, for he sayth, he neuer deliuered any thing to any of my Lady *B*. Gentlewomen. And for his faithfull seruice to her Maiestie, I haue to shewe vnder his owne hande, the penaltie he putteth him selfe too, if any vniust seruice can be layde to his charge.

By this time, the Bell rung for all the

D

THE ENGLISHE

Studentes to come to Supper, which made the Preest to staye at this Periadus, else he would haue continued in discourse, I know not how long: for what with the seueral charges wherwith he sounded me, my care styl how to shape a sufficient aunswer, and the tediousnesse of his tale, mixed with so many woordes, farre distaunt / from ciuill and duetifull regarde, he [19 was not so readie to goe to his Supper, as I was glad for that tyme to breake off company.

So after certaine familiar behauiour, vsed betweene him and I, he glad to see me at *Rome*, and well hoping in shorte time to make me a newe man, I appliable with thankes, for euerie thing, for that it stoode with wisedome to accept all thing: he went into the *Refectorium*, which is the name of their dining Hall, & I to the Chamber appointed for me and my fellow, whome I found there sitting with Doctor *Morris*, staying my comming, that we might sup togeather, which in deede we did. Maister *Morris* vsing vs verie courteouslie, passing away the supper time with much variety of talke, among which, Maister Doctor sayde his pleasure of diuers persons in *England*: which, for that it would rather checke modestie, then challenge any respect of honestie, I admit it to silence, the talke beeing so broade, that it would stand as a blemish to my Booke.

ROMAINE LYFE

In what manner our English men passe away their time in the Colledge, the orders of the house, and other thinges to be regarded.

Chap. 3.

IT is vnpossible for me, to note down halfe the speeches, that passed between yᵉ Schollers and me, as also my fellowe: but as for that was vsed to him, I could sildome come acquainted with all, except I had stoode by & heard it, for either they had fullie perswaded him, or he ioyned / into consent with them: so that he would [20 neuer report any thing that had passed betweene them, he lyked so well of euerie thing. But letting these matters passe a while, I thinke it expedient heere to set downe, before I goe any farder, the orders vsed in the Englishe Colledge, how the English men spende the time there, and within what compasse they limitte them selues, which so breeflie as I can, I will passe ouer.

The Englishe Colledge, is a house bothe large and fayre, standing in the way to the Popes Pallace, not farre from the Castle *Sante*

<small>The place where the Englishe Colledge standeth in *Roome*.</small>

Angello: in the Colledge, the Schollers are deuided, by certaine nũber into euery Chãber, as in some foure, in some six, or so many as the Rector thinketh cõuenient, as well for the health of the Schollers, as the troubling not much roome. Euerie man hath his Bed proper to him selfe, which is, two little Trestles, with fowre or fiue boordes layde along ouer them, and thereon a quilted Mattresse, as we call it in *England*, which euerie morning after they are rysen, they folde vp their sheetes hansomelie, laying them in the middest of the Bed, & so rowle it vp to one ende, couering it with the Quilt, that is their Couerlet all the night time.

The order for the English mennes lodging.

First in the morning, he that is the Porter of the Colledge, ringeth a Bell, at the sound whereof euerie Student ariseth, and turneth vp his Bed, as I haue sayde before. Not long after, the Bell ringeth againe, when as euerie one presentlie kneeling on his knees, prayeth for the space of halfe an howre: at which time, the Bell beeing touled againe, they arise and bestowe a certaine time in Studie, euerie one hauing his Deske, Table, & Chayre to him selfe verie orderlie, and all the time of Studie, silence is vsed of euerie one in the Chãber, not one offering molestation in speeche to an other.

The orders obserued by the Schollers, euerie morning.

The time of Studie expired, the Bell calleth

ROMAINE LYFE 31

them / from their Chambers, downe into [21] the *Refectorium*: where euerie one taketh a glasse of Wine, and a quarter of a Manchet, & so he maketh his *Collatione*. Soone after, the Bel is knouled againe, when as the Studẽts two & two togeather, walke to the *Romaine* Colledge, which is the place of Schoole or instruction: where euerie one goeth to his ordinarie Lecture, some to Diuinitie, some to Phisique, some to Logique, & some to Rhetorique. There they remaine the Lecture time, which beeing done, they returne home to the Colledge againe: where they spend the time tyll dinner, in walking and talking vp and downe the Gardens.

And an order there is appointed by the Rector and the *Iesuites*, and obeyed by all the Studentes, that who soeuer dooth not in the morning turne vp his Bed hansomlie, or is not on his knees at prayer time, or heareth not Masse before he goe to Schoole, or after he comes home, but forgetteth it: or else if he goe foorth, and put not the Peg at his name in the Table. For there is a Table hangeth by the doore, which hath a long Box adioyned to it, wherein lyeth a great company of wooden Pegges, and against the name of euerie Scholler written in the Table (which is obserued by order of the Alphabet) there is a hole made: wherein, such as haue occasion to

The diuersitie of penaunce adioyned the Englishe Studentes: which they must doo openlie in the Hall, at dinner tyme.

goe abroade, must duelie put a Peg, to giue knowledge who is abroade, and who remaineth within.

Beside, diuers other orders they haue for slight matters, the neglecting whereof, is publique penaunce at dinner time: when as all the Studentes are placed at the Tables, such as haue so transgressed, goeth vp into the Pulpit (which standeth there, because one readeth all the dinner tyme) and there he sayeth: Because I haue not fulfilled this or that, whatsoeuer order it be that he hath broken, I am adioyned such a penaunce. / [22 Eyther to kneele in the middest of the Hall on his bare knees, and there to say his Beades ouer: Or to say certaine *Pater nosters*, and Aue *Marias*: Or to stand vpright and haue a dishe of potage before him on the grounde, and so to bring vp euerie spoonfull to his mouth: Or to loose, either one or two or three of his dishes appointed for his dinner: Or to stand there all dinner time, & eate no meate: and diuers other, which according as it is, either afterwarde he hath his dinner or supper, or else goes without it. And all these penaunces I haue beene forced to do, for that I was alway apt to breake one order or other. As for the priuate penaunces, it shall not be greatly amisse to rehearse them heere too: so long I shall desire you to stay, from hearing the

[margin: All these I haue beene forced to do, albeit it were with an yll will.]

manner of the Students dinner. The priuate Penaunces, are appointed by the ghostly Father at Confession: which are fulfilled without publique knowledge of the cause, and likewise of the person. If his penaunce be, to whip him selfe openlie in the Hall at dinner time: then the Rector ordereth it after this manner, that he shall not be knowen, to be reproched by any of his felowes, or that they shall certainlie saye, it is such a one. At the dinner or supper, that this penaunce is to be accomplished, the Rector causeth seuen or eight to keepe their Chambers, and commonly but one that time in a Chamber: their doores must be made fast to them, & they, not so much as looke out at their windowe, to see from which Chamber he comes that dooth the penaunce. When they are all set at the Tables, he commeth in, cloathed in a Canuas vesture downe to the grounde, a hood of the same on his head, with two holes where through he hath sight, and a good bigge round place bare, against the middest of his backe: in this order he goeth vp and downe the Hall, whipping him selfe at that bare place, in somuch, that the blood dooth trickle on the ground after him. / The whip hath [23 a verie short handle, not much aboue a handfull long, and fortie or fiftie Cordes at it, about the length of halfe a yarde: with a great

The priuate penaunces, which are appointed by the ghostly Father.

The whipping them selues, publiquelie at dinner.

THE ENGLISHE

many hard knots on euerie Corde, and some of the whippes hath through euerie knot at the ende crooked wiers, which will teare the fleshe vnmercifullie.

<small>The māner of the Iesuits whips wherewith they whip themselues.</small>

The *Iesuites* haue, some of them, to whip them selues, whips with Cordes of wier, wherewith they will beate them selues, tyl with too much effuse of blood, they be readie to giue vp the ghost. And this they will doo in their Chambers, either before a *Crucifix*, or the image of our Ladie, turning their backes when they bleede towarde the Image, that it may see them. One of the *Iesuites*, because they could neuer gette me to whip my selfe,

<small>Joel. 2.13. Psal.51.17.</small>

(for that I well knewe God sayde: *Rent your hearts, and not your skin*: And that, *A contrite and sobbing heart, is more acceptable to God, then a bleeding body*,) tooke me once with him into his Chamber, saying: I should see (because I was so fearefull) what he would inflict vpon his owne body. So when he was vnapparelled, he tooke a whip, the Cords whereof was wier, & before the Picture of our Lady, he whipped him selfe verie greeuouslie, saying: *Sancta Maria mater Dei, suscipe dolorem meum: Sancta Maria mater Dei, accipe Flagitium meum: Et ora pro me, nunc et in hora mortis:* Which is as much to say, *Saint Marie mother of God, receiue my dolor: Saint Marie mother of God, accept my whipping, and pray for*

<small>The exāple one of the Iesuites gaue me, to whip my selfe.</small>

<small>O monstrous ignoraunce.</small>

me, now and in the howre of death. These, with other like woordes, he vsed to the Picture a great many times: and then he went to the *Crucifix,* which stoode vpon his Deske, and whipping him selfe styll, he sayde these, or the verie lyke woordes. *O Iesu, obtestetur te virgo gloriosa Maria mater, quæ (quod pro certo noui) pro me nunc tecum agit. Flagitij tui, sanguinolenti tui sudoris, Crucis tuæ, mortis ac passionis tuæ, pro | me passæ memoria, ad hoc me* [24 *faciendum impulit: eo quod perpessus sis, his decies pro me grauiora:* In English thus. *O Iesus, be thou intreated by that glorious virgin thy mother, who I am sure at this time maketh intercession to thee for me. The remembraunce of thy whipping, bloody sweat, Crosse, death and passion, maketh me do this, in somuch as thou hast suffered ten times more for me.*

<small>Egregious impudency.</small>

In these and such like acclamations, he continued whipping him selfe, almost the space of halfe an howre, bleeding so sore, as it greeued me verie much to see him. Afterward, he willed me to trie it once, and I shoulde not finde any paine in it, but rather a pleasure. For (quoth he) if Christe had his fleshe rent and torne with whips, his handes and feete nayled to the Crosse, his precious side gored with a Launce, his head so pricked with a Crowne of thorne, that his deere blood ran trilling downe his face, and all this for you:

why should you feare to put your body to any torment, to recompence him that hath done so much for you? I desired him to beare with me a while, for I was not indued with that strength and fortitude, as to abide and suffer the paines he did: but yet in time I doubted not, to fulfill any thing on my body, he would commaund me. My aunswer pleased him indifferentlie, so I left him in his Chamber, and went downe, lamenting to see a spectacle of so great follie.

Diuersity of penaunces, giuen them, all by their ghostly Cōfessor.

Now as for the other penaunces, as they be diuers, so be they diuers wayes fulfilled, eyther by Fasting, wearing a shyrt of heaire, trudging to the seuen Churches, lying vpon the bare boardes, going into the darke vautes vnder the ground, or traueling on Pilgrimage, and a number more, which exceedeth my memorie to vnfolde, they haue amongst them, as there be diuers can beare me witnesse, and some of them my Confessor / hath con- [25 strayned me to doo.

The maner of the English mens dinner.

Returne we now to the Students, who beeing come from the schooles, and haue recreated them selues some what, either in the house or in the Gardens: are now at the sound of the Bel come into the *Refectorium* to dinner. The custome is, that dayly two of the Studentes take it by turnes, to serue all the other at ye Table, who to helpe them, haue the

ROMAINE LYFE

Butler, the Porter, and a poore *Iesuite*, that looketh to all the Schollers necessaries, to bring them their cleane shirtes, and foreseeeth, that neither their Gownes, Cassocks, Dublets, Breeches, Hose nor shooes want mending. These bring in their hands, eche of them a round boorde, which hath a staffe about halfe a yarde long, made fast through the middle of it: and round about that boord is set little Saucers, wherin the Cooke shareth euery man a little quantity, which they bring, and holde ouer the Table, when as euerie man taketh his owne messe.

As for their fare, trust me it is very fine and delicate, for euery man hath his owne Trentcher, his Manchet, knife, spoone, and forke layde by it, & then a fayre white napkin couering it, with his glasse and pot of wine set by him. And the first messe, or *Antepast* (as they call it) that is brought to the Table, is some fine meat to vrge them haue an appetite: as sometime the Spanish *Anchouies*, and sometime stued Prunes and Raysons of the Sun togeather, hauing such fine tarte sirope made to them, as I promise you a weake stomacke would very wel digest them. The second, is a certaine messe of potage of that Countrey manner, no meat sod in them, but are made of diuers thinges, whose proper names I doo not remember: but me thought they were

<small>The variety of dishes, and daintinesse of the Englishe mens fare.</small>

bothe good and wholsome. The thirde, is boylde meate, as Kid, Mutton, Chickin, and such like: euerie man a pretie modicum of eche thing. The fourth, is rosted meat, / [26 of the daintiest prouision that they can get, and sometime stewde and bakte meate, according as pleaseth Maister Cooke to order it. The first and last, is some time Cheese, some time preserued conceytes, some tyme Figges, Almonds and Raysons, a Limon and Sugar, a Pomegranate, or some such sweete geere: for they knowe that Englishmen looueth sweete meates.

The order that one of the Schollers obserueth, reading all the dinner tyme.

And all the dinner whyle, one of the Schollers, according as they take it by weeklie turne, readeth: first a Chapter of their Bible, and then in their *Martirilogium*, he readeth the Martirdome of some of the Saintes, as Saint *Fraunces*, Saint *Martin*, Saint *Longinus*, that thrust the Speare into Christes side, Saint *Agatha*, Saint *Barbara*, Saint *Cecilia*, and diuers other: among whome they haue imprinted the Martirdome of Doctor *Storie*, the two *Nortons*, *Iohn Felton* and others, calling them by the name of Saintes, who were heere executed at Tiborne for high treason.

The dinner done, they recreate them selues for ye space of an howre, & then the Bell calleth them to theyr Chãbers, where they staye a while, studying on their Lectures

giuen them in the forenoone: anon the Bel
sūmoneth them to Schoole again, where they
stay not past an howre, but they returne home   They
againe, and so soone as they be come in, they   haue
goe into the *Refectorium*, and there euerie one   enough,
hath his glasse of wine, and a quarter of a   foure
Manchet againe, according as they had in the   day.
morning.

Then they depart to their Chambers, from
whence at conuenient time they are called to
exercise of disputation: the Diuines to a
Iesuite appointed for them, and euerie Studie
to a seuerall *Iesuite*, where they continue the
space of an howre, and afterwarde tyll supper
tyme, they are at theyr recreation. /   [27

After Supper, if it be in winter time, they   Their
goe with the *Iesuites*, and sit about a great fire   exercise
talking, and in all their talke, they striue who   Supper.
shall speake wurst of her Maiesty, of some of
her Councell, of some Bishop heere, or such
lyke: so that the *Iesuites* them selues, will often
take vp their hands and blesse them selues, to
heare what abhominable tales they will tell
them. After they haue talked a good while,
the Bell calleth them to their Chambers, the
Porter going from Chamber to Chãber, &
lighteth a Lampe in euerie one: so when the
Schollers come, they alight their Lampes, lay
downe their Beddes, and goe sit at their
Deskes and studie a little, tyll the Bell ringes,

40 *THE ENGLISHE*

when euerie one falles on his knees to Prayers. Then one of the Preestes in the Chamber, as in euerie Chamber there is some, beginneth the Latin Letany, all the Schollers in the Chamber aunswering him: and so they spend the time tyll the Bell ringes againe, which is for euerie one to goe to bed.

¶ *Other matters of our Englishe Studentes in the Colledge, their dayes of recreation at their vineyarde, their walke to the seuen Churches, a report of some of the Romish Reliques, and other thinges concerning their behauiour.*

Chap. 4. / [28

THe English Studentes euerie thirde or fowrth day, goe not to the Schooles, but haue accesse abroade, to sport and delight them selues: sometime they walke to theyr Vineyarde, and the *Iesuites* with them, where they passe away the day in diuers disportes, what game, what toy any one can deuise, they altogeather in pastime ioyne to performe it.

ROMAINE LYFE 41

An other day they goe to the seuen Churches, which according as I remember their names, I will heere set them downe. S. *Peters*, S. *Paules*, S. *Iohn Lateranes*, S. *Maria maiore*, S. *Croce*, S. *Laurences*, S. *Sebastianes*. In all these Churches, there be diuers Reliques, which make them haunted of a meruailous multitude of people: whereby the lazie lurden Friers that keepe the Churches, gettes more ritches, then so many honest men should doo. For eyther at the comming into the Church, or else at the Aultar where the Reliques be, there standeth a Basen, and the people cast money therein, with very great liberality. And there standeth a Frier, with a forked sticke in his hand, and thervpon he taketh euerie bodies Beades, that layes them on the Aultar, and then he wipes them along a great proportioned thing of Christall and Golde, wherein are a number of rotten bones, which they make the people credite to be the bones of Saintes: so wiping them along the outside of this Tabernacle, the Beades steale a terrible deale of holynesse out of those bones, and God knowes, the people thinke they doo God good seruice in it: Oh monstrous blindnesse.

But because euery good Subiect may see into the Ro- / mishe iuglinges, and per- [29 ceyue the subtiltie of Anti-christe the eldest

marginalia:
The seuen Churches in Roome, wherto they goe on pylgrimage.

A craftie kinde of coosonage, wherby the ignorant people are beguiled.

childe of hell: I will rehearse some of these Reliques, as many of them as I can possiblie call to my remembraunce.

A breefe rehearsall of some of the Romishe Reliques, whereby the Pope deceiueth a number, and hath good gaines, to the maintenaunce of his pompe.

In Saint Peters Church.

<small>The Popes brasē Rock, taken for the Rock Christ spake off.</small>

AS we enter into the Court before Saint *Peters* Church, there standeth the forme of a Rock made of brasse, an old & aunciēt thing: the which is kept there, that the ignoraunt people should beleeue that to be the Rock, which our Sauiour spake off to *Peter*, when as vpon *Peters* confessing him to be, *Christe the sonne of the liuing God:* he aunswered. *Vpon this Rock will I builde my Church*, which Rock he meant by him selfe, and not by *Peter*. This peece of brasse they make the ignorant to beleeue to be that Rock, and therfore a nūber as they goe into the Church, fall downe on their knees, and worship this brasen Rock with their prayers.

<small>Math.16. 16.18.</small>

<small>The halfe bodies of S. *Peter* and *Paule*.</small>

Going thorowe the Church, we come to a Chappell, wherin is an high Altar, wheron standeth a Picture of S. *Peter* and S. *Paul:* within that Altar, they say, lyeth halfe the bodyes of these two Apostles and Saints, and therfore that Aultar is daylie worshipped.

Comming back againe into the Church, we come to a square Aultar, wherin (say they) is the head of ye Speare that was thrust into our Sauiours side: but the point therof, is broken off, and is in an other place. And in the / [30 same Aultar, is ye Hãdkercher which Christe wiped his face with all, when he caried his Crosse sweating, & left the perfect print therof on ye cloath: this is called *Vultus sanctus.* How this aultar is honored, you shal read more in the Chapter, which talketh of the *Flagellante* night.

<small>The speare that was thrust into Christes side, and the handkercher wherewith he wiped his face, when he carried his Crosse.</small>

What other Reliques be in this Church, I certainlie knowe not, but they say there is the bodies of diuers Saintes: whose names because I can not remember, I will let passe, because I will not be founde in an vntrueth.

In Saint Paules *Church.*

IN this Church, vnder the high Aultar, is sayde to be the other halfe of the bodies of S. *Peter* and *Paule*: this Aultar is likewise adored with meruailous reuerence.

<small>The other halfe of S. *Peter* and *Paule.*</small>

E

44 THE ENGLISHE

Three leapes of S. *Paules* head made three Fountains.

Not farre from this Church, there is a place called *Tre-Fontana*, at this place they say Saint *Paule* was beheaded: and when his head was cutte off, it leaped three times, and in those places where it leapt, there sprung vp presentlie three Fountaines, there is great deuotion likewise vsed at this place.

In Saint Iohn Lateranes *Church*.

The stone whereon the Cock crewe, when *Peter* denyed Christe.

AS we come first to the little Chappelles before the Church (wherein, they say, our Lady hath beene diuers times seene and therefore hath left such holinesse there, as they pray there a good while) there standeth a round pyller of Stone, seeming to be but latelie made, & on this Stone, say they, the Cock stoode and crowed, at what time *Peter* denied *Christe*: & therfore they doo vse to kisse it, make courtesie to it, & rub their Beades on it. /

The rings wherin the Iewes set their Banners, when Christ was crucified.

Neere to this Stone, is a broade gate, beeing the entraunce into the aforesayde Chappelles, and on the one side of this gate, there is two round Ringes of Iron, whereon sometime a gate hath beene hanged, to open and shut: in these Ringes, say they, the Iewes did stick Banners, all the while that Christe was crucified, and therfore for the holinesse of them, they will drawe their Beades thorowe the sayd Rings, and kisse them when they haue so done.

From thence we goe to a fayre large place, in the middest whereof standeth a Font, wherein, they saye, *Constantinus Magnus* was christened: in this Font euerie yeere on *Easter* euen, they doo christen Iewes, such as doo chaunge to their Religion. For there is a certaine place appointed for Sermons, whereat y̓ Iewes whether they will or no, must be present, because one of their own *Rabines* preacheth to them, to conuert them, as him selfe hath beene a great while.

The Font wherein Constantinus Magnus was Christened.

In *Roome*, the Iewes haue a dwelling place within them selues, beeing locked in their streetes by gates on either side, and the Romaines euerie night keepeth the keyes: all the day time they goe abroade in the Cittie, and will buie the oldest apparell that is, an olde Cloke Dublet, or Hose, that a man would thinke not woorth a penny, of the Iewes you may haue y̓ quantity of fowre or fiue shillings for them. Now, that the Iewes may be knowne from any other people, euerie one weareth a yellow Cap or Hat, and if he goe abroade without it, they will vse him verie yll fauouredlie.

In this order they come to the Sermon, and when any of them dooth chaunge his Faith:

he taketh his yellowe Cap or Hat off from his head, and throwes it away with great violence, then will a hundred offer him a blacke Cap or a Hat, and greatlie reioyce that / they haue [32 so wun him. All his riches he then must forsake, y^t goes to the Popes vse, beeing one of his shiftes: and to this aforesayd Font he is brought, clothed all in white, a white Cap, a white Cloke, & euery thinge white about him, with a holy Candle burning, that he beareth in his hand. Then is he there baptized by an English man, who is named Bishop *Goldwell*, sometime the Bishop of S. *Asaph* in Wales: he hath thys office, maketh all the English Priests in the Colledge, and liueth there among the *Theatines* verye pontificallye. After ye Iewes be thus baptized, they be brought into the Church, and there they see the hallowing of the *Paschall*, which is a mighty great wax Taper: and then a deuise (wherin is inclosed a number of Squibs) is shot off, when thorow all the Church they then cry, *Sic transit gloria Mundi*. From thence they goe to a Colledge, which the Pope hath erected for such Iewes, as in this manner turn to his religion: there they stay a certain time, and afterward they be turned out, to get their liuing as they can, none of their former riches they must haue again, for that goes to the maintenance of the Popes pontificallitie.

Marginalia:
Bishoppe *Goldwell* baptizeth the Iewes in Roome.

Hallowing of the Paschall Candle.

This aforesaide Font is a holy thing, and there must prayers be likewise saide.

From this Font we goe vp into a fayre Chappell, wherein is an Aultar dedicated to our Lady, in golde and sumptuous showes surpassing, and all about the Chappel are hanged little wooddden Pictures, Tapers, and wax Candles, which are the Pilgrimes vowes to our Lady, and there they leaue them to honour her. Heere must be vsed great deuotion. *Our Ladies holy Chappell.*

From thence we goe into an old roome, wherein is an old Wall standing along in the midst of this roome, and in this Wall is three old doores, hauing paynting on them that is not verye olde: thorowe one of these / [32 doores, they say, Christ went in to iudgement, when he came backe from iudgement, he went thorow the second, and thorow the third to be whipped: these doores are worshipped euery day. *The three holy doores.*

From thence we goe a long thorow an old Gallerye, and there is a fayre payre of stayres of stone, that commeth vp into this Gallerie, beeing in number of steps, about foure or fiue & twenty: vp these stayres they saye Christ went to iudgement, & as he came back again, *The holy stayres that Christ went vp to iudgement on.*

he let fall a drop of blood on one of the steps, ouer yᵉ which place (because the people with kissing it and rubbing it with their Beades, haue fretted a deepe hole in yᵉ stone) is made a little Iron grate. The people must neither goe vp nor down these stayres, on their feete, but creepe them vpon their knees, and on euery step say a *Pater noster* & an *Aue Maria:* so yᵗ with the number that creepe vp & down these stayres dayly, they are kept as cleane, as yᵉ fine houses in London, wher you may see your face in the boordes. These stayres haue no small reuerence.

The vaile of the Temple, that rent in the middest.

Neere to the head of these stayres, on eyther side of the Gallery, there is in the Walles two halfe pillers of stone, much like to Alablaster: which they say, to be the vayle of the Temple that rent in the middest, when Christ yeelded vp the Ghost, vpon these two halfe pillers, they rub their Beads, in signe of great deuotiõ.

The Piller that Christe was whipped at.

Somewhat neere to these halfe pillers, there is a long Marble piller, at which piller, they saye, Christ was fast bound, when he was whipped in *Pilates* hall. This piller is much adored.

Some of the Milke of our

Hard by, we goe, into a little Chapell, which hath a very rich & costly Aultar, wherin they

say to be, some of the Milke that came out of   Ladies
our Ladyes brests, and as yet remaineth pure   brests.
and sweete. To this Relique is / vsed [34
meruailous worship.

And in the same Chappell, hard by the   A peece
doore as wee come in, there hangeth tyed with   of the
an Yron chaine a peece of wood, which is   Crosse,
                                               whereon
crossed euery way with diuers plates of Yron: the good
this peece of wood, they name to bee a peece   Theefe
of the crosse, whereon the theefe was hanged, was
to whom our Sauiour sayde. *This day thou shalt* hanged.
be with me in Paradise. To this is giuen much
deuotion.

Beneath in the Church.

IN the Church at the high Aultar, there is as   The first
they say, the first Shirt, that our Lady made   Shirt that
for Christe, when he was young.   was made
                                                for
                                                Christe.

In the same Aultar, are the two sculs or   The heads
scalps, of the heads of S. *Peter*, and S. *Paule*,   of Saint
                                            Peter and
with the heire as yet on them: which are set   S. *Paule*.
in Golde and Siluer very costlye.

There is also a glasse viall, which is full as   A glasse
they say, of the blood of our Sauiour, that ran viall, full
                                                 of the
out of his precious side hanging on ye Crosse: blood of
the people whẽ this is showẽ, will take their   Christ.
hands, & hold the palmes of thẽ toward the
glasse, and then rub all their face with their

50 THE ENGLISHE

hands, with the great holines they receiue from the Glasse.

<small>A peece of Christes Cote, with his bloode yet fresh on it.</small>

Then ther is a peece of Christes Cote without seame, and it is the part of the Cote, which when it was turned downe ouer his body, that he should be whipped, ye blood did trickle downe vpon: and vpon this peece of his Cote, say they, ye blood yet remaineth as fresh, as it was ye first day when it fell on it. This is a meruailous precious Relique too.

<small>The chaine wherewith S. *Iohn* was led to *Ephesus*.</small>

Likewise there is ye whole chaine of Iron, wherwith S. *Iohn* the Euangelist, was led bound to *Ephesus*: thys Chaine is a little olde one, I am sure little aboue halfe a yarde long./

<small>One of the Nailes that nailed Christ on the Crosse.</small>

There is also one of the Nayles, where-[35 with our Sauiour Christ was nayled on the Crosse: and it hath the blood yet fresh vpon it.

<small>A parte of the Crowne of Thorne.</small>

And among all the rest, there is a great portion or quantitie of the Crowne of Thorne, wherewith they say our Sauiour was crowned.

Diuers other Reliques there bee in that Church, which I cannot now very perfectly remember: but these I am certaine they make the people beleeue to be there, for I haue stoode by amonge a multitude of

people, that come thither to see them on the
day they are showen, and there haue I heard
all these named: almost all the English
Students can beare me witnesse, for I haue
gon in their company, as it is a custome and
an order among them, to goe from Church to
Church all the Lent time, to the *Stations* as
they call them, and then each day in Lent,
one Church or other hath their Reliques
abroade to be seene. And thẽ they tell the
people, this is the Reliques of such a Saint,
and this is such a holy and blessed thing: but
they be either couered with Gold, Siluer, or
Christall, so that we can not tell whether there
be any thing within or no, except it bee sometime in a broade Christall Tabernacle, and
there you shall see a company of rotten bones,
God knowes of what they be.

In Saint Maria Maiore.

THere is an olde rotten Crib or Manger, The Manger
wherin say they, our Sauiour lay, be- wherin
tweene the Oxe, and the Asse, when the Christ
Sheepheards came to honour & reuerence layde.
him. This is a thing highly honored.

There is likewise *Arons* rod, as they call it, *Arons* rod.
which / is in the forme of a Bishops staffe: a [36
holy Relique.

Heire of our Ladies head.

There is also of the heire, that grew on our Ladies head: this is there reserued richly, and worshipped for a singuler Relique.

S. Thomas his finger.

There is the forme of a finger in Siluer, wherein, say they, is the finger of S. *Thomas*, which he thrust into the side of Christ: this is no simple Relique.

The poynte of the speare that was thrust into Christes side.

There is the point of the head of a Speare, which they say, to be broken off from the Speare, that was thrust into our Sauiours side on the Crosse: a Relique of no small worshipp.

Some of the thirtye pence, for which Iudas betrayed Christe.

There is also certaine peeces of Mony, which they name to be of those thirty pence, which *Iudas* receiued when he betrayed his Maister, wherwith (after he had hanged him selfe) they bought a feeld, called: *The feeld of bloode*. These are Reliques of great estemation.

A peece of Christes Crosse.

There is likewise an old rotten peece of wood, which they make the people to thinke, to be a peece of ye Crosse whereon Christ was crucified: to see this Relique, the people will come creeping on their knees, and behaue them selues with meruailous deuoutnes.

There is also certaine of the Thornes,

ROMAINE LYFE 53

which sometime, as they say, were on the Crowne of Thorne, wherewith our Sauiour Christ was crowned: Reliques of great authoritye among them.

<small>Thornes of the crowne of Thornes.</small>

In Sancta Croce.

THere is an other of the Nayles, wherewith Christ was nayled on the Crosse: and as they say, ye blood / still fresh vpon it.

<small>An other of the nayles wherewith Christ was nayled.</small>

[37

There is also three or foure of the pence, which *Iudas* receiued for the betraying of his Maister Christ.

<small>More of *Iudas* pence.</small>

There is a good big peece of wood, which they likewise say to be a peece of the Crosse, whereon Christ was crucified.

<small>More of the Crosse.</small>

There is a Whippe, which they report to be one of those whips, wherwith Christ was whipped in *Pilates* Hall. This is a holy and very precious Relique.

<small>One of the whyppes wherewith Christ was whipped.</small>

There is a Tabernacle of Christall, the Pillers therof are of siluer, wherin is diuers old rotten bones, which they say to be the bones of Saintes, and holye Martires.

<small>Reliques of Saintes.</small>

In Saint Lauraunces.

The stone whereon S. Laraunce was broiled.

THere is made faste in a Wall, a great Marble stone, about two yardes in length, and a yarde in bredth, which is closed in with a grate of Iron: vppon this stone they say, S. *Lauraunce* was broyled. This is a Relique much set by.

The Grediron wheron S. Laraunce was broiled.

There also they say to be the Grediron whereon S. *Lauraunce* was broyled: but that I neuer sawe, therefore I will not make any certaine report thereof.

The head of Saint Lauraunce.

There at the high Aultar, they say the heade of S. *Lauraunce* is, which they haue set in Siluer meruailous costly. / [38

In Saint Sebastians.

The body of Saint Sebastian.

THere vnder the High Aulter, they say lyeth the body of S. *Sebastian*, to whose shrine they offer very much worshippe.

At all these seuen Churches, there are a number more Reliques then I can well remember, which maketh the people to resort to them almost daylye: and our Englishmen, they are as zealous in these matters as the best, and beleeue that those Reliques are the very certaine thinges whereof they beare the name, so great is their blindnes and want of fayth.

To these places they trudge commonly once

euery weeke, sometime twise, or as the *Iesuites* thinke it conuenient: but when they haue beene at these seuen Churches, and honoured al these paltry Reliques, they thinke they haue doone a moste blessed and acceptable seruice to God.

There are Reliques beside these, at most of the other Churches and Chappelles, but what they be, I doo not as nowe remember: yet thus much I can say, that when the *Station* hath beene at Saint *Appolonias*, all the way as we goe, the streetes are full almoste of lame and diseased people, who, when they desire an almes of the passers by, say, they will pray to S. *Appolonia* for their teeth, that shee will keepe them from ye toothache, or any other paine that may happen to their teeth. This they doo, because they report, that S. *Appolonia* being Martired, had all her teeth by violence plucked out of her head: and therfore they imagin, that she can defend any body from hauing any payne in their teeth.

Prayer to S. Appolonia. for the toothache.

Likewise S. *Agatha*, whose brestes they say, were clipped off with a payre of tonges, made red hot in the fire: to her they will pray (if ye people will giue thẽ any money) y^t any Woman passing by them, this Saint will not suffer her to haue any payne in her brestes. /

Prayer to S. Agatha for womens brestes.

Other of their Saintes, who had any [39 thing ministred by way of torment, eyther on their heade, armes, body, legs, or feete: because the people shall giue them somewhat, these Beggers wil pray to anye of those Saints, to defende thẽ from payne in any such place of theyr bodye.

<small>A cunning shift of Beggers.</small>

Now some lazie Fryer, or some other craftye companion, who will not take so much paynes as to begge, but that he will compell the people to giue him somewhat: he getteth a *Pax*, and euery one that commeth by him, must make homage to it, come and kisse it, and giue him some Mony, ere he goe any further. This fellow standeth as Maister of the Beggers, and all these knaueries, and an infinite number more, are our Englishmen so insolent, both to like and allow off.

<small>A commaunding Begger.</small>

And now seeing I am among the Popes Pageants, I will blaze a little more of his holy Hell: that those (to whose handes this my Booke shall happen to come, and are by some of our secrete seducing Priestes anye thing mooued that way) may beholde the egregious follies and deuillish drifts, whereby God is dispised, and mẽ too much wilfully blinded. So that, turning to the bare and naked trueth, which craueth neither shadowe nor any coullored deuise: they may vomit vppe that Antechrist and his abhominable inuentions, and cleaue onely to that which God him selfe hath commaunded. /   [40

ROMAINE LYFE

¶ *A breefe discourse of their darke Vautes vnderneath the ground, and how they beguile a number by them. Of the Pilgrimage to S. Iames in Gallitia, to S. Maria di Loreto, to Saint Clare at Mount Faulcon, & other places of like holines.*

Chap. 5.

Mong a nūber of their inuentions, to vpholde and maintaine their wicked dealings: they haue certaine Vautes vnderneath the groūd, wherin they say, how in the tyme that the persecuting Emperours lyued in *Roome*, the Christians were glad to hide them selues: and there they liued many yeeres, hauing no foode or nourishment to maintaine them, but onelie that they were fed by Angelles. Some time Christe him selfe came amongst them, and he fed them by his heauenlie Deitie. When as he could not come, but was busied about other affaires: he sent his Mother the Virgin *Marie* to them. At other times, the Archangell *Michaell*, the Angell *Gabriell*, or one Angell or other, was still sent vnto them: and Saintes that were

Marke this good Reader, & thinke well theron.

58 *THE ENGLISHE*

liuing on earth, came daylie and preached to them. This our English men hath tolde to me & other, at diuers times: yea, and when they haue seene me to offer doubt of those matters, they haue beene ready to sweare it to be certaine and true.

The Vaut at Saint Pancratias Church.

At a Church there called Saint *Pancratia*, there is a Vaute, whereinto I haue gone with the *Iesuites* of the / Englishe Colledge and [41 the Studentes: and there they haue shewed me in diuers places made on eyther side in the Vaut as we goe, that there lay such a Saint, and there lay such an other, there they were buried, & none was there, but they were all Saintes. Then (hauing euerie one of vs a wax light in our hands, because it is vnpossible to see any light in the Vaute, and for those lights, the Friers that keepe the Church must haue money, which we put into a Basen, that standeth at the going downe into the Vaute) they looke on the ground vnder their feete as they goe: and if they chaunce to finde a bone (as some sure are throwen in of purpose, to deceyue the people) whether it be of a Dog, a Hog, a Sheepe, or any Beast, they can tell presentlie what Saints bone it was, either Saint *Fraunces*, Saint *Anthonie*, Saint *Blase*, or some other Saint that pleaseth them to name. Then must no body touch it, without he be a Preest, and it must be brought home for an especiall Relique: and thus (sauing your reuerence) encreaseth the genealogie of the holy Reliques in *Roome*.

In this aforesayde Vaute of Saint *Pancratia*, as one of the English Preestes in the Colledge gaue me to vnderstand, there was some time a *Franciscan* Frier, who hauing long time liued among his brethren in the Monasterie, in chastitie of life, and deuoutnes in Religion: walking one day without *Roome*, Saint *Fraunces* appeared to him in his Friers Cowle, and calling him by his name, sayd vnto him. I knowe my good Brother, thou hast long thus liued in my holy order, and hast obeyed me in euerie thing: therfore I will, that thou be no longer a mortall man, but a Saint. And from this time foreward, thou shalt leaue thy Cloister, & go to the Vaute vnder the Church of Saint *Pancratia*: where thou shalt be woorshipped of euerie one that commeth into the sayde Vaute, and to them thou shalt giue the bones and Reliques of holie and blessed Saintes, which they in their Churches shal adore with great reuerẽce: what thou wilt haue, shall be done, and what thou wilt not, shall not be done.

After these woordes, Saint *Fraunces* vanished from him, & he went home to the Monastery, to tell his Brethren what had happened: soone after, with burning Tapers,

A meruailous history and one of the Romish miracles.

and great showes of holines they brought him to the Vaute of Saint *Pancratia*, wherin beeing entred, they found a seate ready prepared for him, which shined as bright as the Sun, so that it dimmed the light of all their Tapers: it was like vnto the Clowdes, verie thick beset with twinkling Starres, and ouer the head of it, it was couered with a goodly Rainbowe. Nothing could be seen wheron this seate depended, it neither touched the groũd, the top of the Vaute ouer head, nor any part of the wall on eyther side, therefore it was supported by Angels, whome though they could not discerne, yet they heard them make verie mellodious hermony, to welcom this Saint to his new seat. Then the Frier beeing bashfull, to see such a glorious seate prouided for him, withdrew him selfe, as though he were vnwoorthy to sit therein: but then out of one of the Clowds stretched a hand (which they sayde to be Christes) wherein they sawe the fresh bleeding wound, beeing pierced thorow with the nayle on the Crosse, and this hand pulled the Frier to the Seat, & placed him very roially therin. At ye sight heerof, all his brethren fell downe & worshipped him, whervpõ, he deliuered vnto euery one of them diuers holy Reliques: as the head of such a Saint, and bones of diuers other Saints, which was put in to his hand to giue them. Some of

Marke this.

O horrible and abhominable blasphemie.

them for pure zeale, would not depart frõ him, but staied there many yeeres, beeing fed & nourished by Angels: the other, to looke to the good ordering of their Monastery, were forced to depart. /   [43

Along time this Saint remained in that Vaute, and many other that came to him, whome he daylie made Saintes: so that, as well on the behalfe of this Saint, as diuers other as good as he, this Vaute is worshipped as though it were a second heauen.

When he had ended this braue notorious Fable, deliuered foorth with farre more reuerend iesture, then I can set downe, or you imagine: he sayde. If a man should tell this to the Heretiques of our Coũtrey, they would strayte way condemne it as a lye & vntrueth: so mightilie dooth the deuill preuayle with them, to deface the daylie miracles showne in the Catholique Church. Trust me (thought I) I know not whether they would esteeme it for a lye or no: but I doo allowe it for one of the notablest lyes that euer I heard in all my life.

O my deere Countreimen, thinke how God hath giuen ouer these men, that repose credite in such abhominable vntruethes: whereby he is robbed of his glory, & the worship which we ought of duetie to giue to him, is bestowed on a rable of rascall Reliques, a dunghil of most irksom & noysom smell, & they themselues become spectacles to the world, following the whore of *Roome*, as her puddle of accursed filthinesse. Their impietie hath pierced the heauens, and offended the Almightie, to see that his Creatures shall thus disdaine their Maker: and therefore, while they are glorying and triumphing in the middest of their wickednesse, he hath throwen them downe, accoumpted them as bastards, & not chyldren, that they might be an example to vs, howe to liue in his feare, and howe to behaue our selues lyke Christians, not to giue his honour to stockes & stones, not to lust after dreames and fantasies of the deuilles inuencion: but whyle we haue the light, to walke as becõmeth the chyldren of light, to keepe our selues true and faithfull Subiectes, to her, by whome we enioy the / [44 light, and to pray to God, to blesse her and vs all, to continue in the light. *Amen*.

I will set downe one discourse more, of an other lyke myracle, done in an other of their Vautes: and then I will trouble you no longer with such friuelous & foolish stuffe, which I will declare euen in the same manner, as a Preest of theirs, as yet not taken, yet he is heere in *England*, tolde me, when he, I, and two of the Schollers more, went into the sayde Vaute.

Without *Roome*, about the distaunce of

halfe a myle from ye Cittie, there is a huge great Vaute, which they call S. *Priscillaes* Grote: and within this Vaute, there is a great many of seuerall places, turning one this way, an other that way, as in one streete, there may be diuers streetes and lanes, turning euerie way. So that when they goe into this Vaute, they tye the ende of a lyne at the going in, and so goe on by the lyne, else they might chaūce to loose them selues, and so misse of their euer comming out againe: or else if they haue not a lyne, they take Chalke with them, and make figures at euerie turning, that at their comming againe, (beeing guided by Torch lyght, for Candles will goe out with the dampe in the Vaute) they may make accoumpt tyll they get foorth, but this is not so ready a way as by the lyne.

An other straunge historie, of a Romishe miracle, doon in the Vaut of Saint Priscilla, without Roome.

One day I was desirous to see this Vaute, for my fellowe *Thomas Nowell*, in the company of the *Iesuites* and the Schollers, had beene therein, and I lying sicke in my Bed, bothe he and they made such a glorious report thereof to me, what a Heauenlie place it was, what a number of Saintes and Martirs had beene buried there, and what precious Reliques was daylie found there: that I verie much desired to see the thing, whereto they gaue such an admirable prayse. For in soothe, my fellow was euen all one with them, his com- / pany was required of euerie one, & [45 he as lewde in speeches against his Countrey as the best: so that I was esteemed I can not tell howe, they would not misdoubt me for my Parents sake, & yet they would giue me many shrewd nips. As when they demaunded any thing of me, as concerning our gratious Princesse, or any of her honourable Councell, I should aunswer: Her Maiestie, God blesse her, or, the right Honourable, such a Noble man, of whom they asked me: wherat they would check me verie much, for vsing any reuerence in naming her Maiesty, or any of the Lords of her honorable Coũcell.

I speake not this good Reader, eyther in pride or brauerie. And this I may say boldlie, for that it is true, as God is my witnes, that in all the time I was amõgst them: I neither offered moitie of misordred or vndecẽt speech, either of her Maiestie, or any Noble man in the Court, no, nor so much as thought yll of any of them, notwithstanding the woordes they vsed, sufficient (had not God ordred all my dooinges) to haue mooued a more stayed man then my selfe to an error. I appeale to God, who knoweth I set downe nothing but trueth, & to him that is my cheefest enimie, if he can iustlie report otherwise by me: for I thanke God, albeit I were so far from my Countrey, he gaue me the grace to consider, I was a Subiect, & I was bound by duety to regard

ROMAINE LYFE

and honour my Prince so long as I liued. And because my aduersaries obiect against me, that I went to Masse, & helped the Preest my selfe to say Masse: so that (say they) who is wurst, I am as euill as he. I aunswer, I did so in deed, for he that is in *Roome*, especially in ye Colledge amõg the Schollers: must liue as he may, not as he will, fauour comes by conformitie, and death by obstinacie. These rash heads beeing in *England*, would doo many goodlie matters at *Roome*, they would tell the Pope of his lasciuious & vnchristian life, the Cardinals of their Sodomiticall sinnes, the Friers of their secret iugling / with the [46 Nunnes, & the Preestes of their painted Purgatorie, their wafer God, and their counterfeit blood in the Challice: all this they would doo, nowe they are in *England*. But I doubt if they were at *Roome*, and behelde the mercilesse tiranny executed on the members of Christe, God hauing not endued them with the spirit of perseueraunce, to suffer and abide the like (for what can this frayle carkase endure, if God doo not say: *I will that thou shalt suffer this?*) I feare me, they would be as ready to doo any thing for the safegard of their liues, as I was. You maye note a speciall example, in these our Countreymen lately executed, that neither their cause was esteemed of God, nor perfectlie perswaded in

The will of God must be done in all thinges.

66   THE ENGLISHE

them selues: yet they would die in a brauerie, to be accoumpted Martyres at *Roome*, and in the middest of their brauerie, all the world might note their false and faynt hearts.

Sherwood, he ranne downe the Ladder, when death should arest him, hauing killed one of his fellowe Papistes. *Campion*, their glorious Captaine, he looked dead in the face, so soone as he sawe the place of Execution, and remained quaking & trembling vnto the death. *Shert*, would haue the people thinke, hee feared not death, and yet he catched holde on the halter, when the Cart was drawne away. *Kirbie*, quaking when he felt the Cart goe away, looked styll how neere the ende of it was, tyl he was quite beside. And *Cottom* dismaying, died trembling & in great feare. These are the Martirs of ye Romish Church, not one of them patient, penitent, nor endued with courage to the extremitie of death: but dismaying, trembling & fearfull, as ye eye witnesses can beare me record. We may therfore wel knowe, y^t a good cause dooth animate ye Martir, which belonging to God: let *Roome*, Hell, & all the deuils set them selues against vs, they cã touch vs no farder, thẽ God wil suffer them. / As Saint *Lauraunce* [47] beeing broiled on the Gridiron, to witnesse the inuincible courage wherewith God endued him, he sayde: *Thou Tiraunt, this side is*

Sherwood, executed in Southwark.

S. Lauraũce.

now roasted enough, turne the other. And Saint *Isidore* likewise sayde to the Tiraunt: *I knowe thou hast no further power ouer me, then my God will suffer thee from abooue.* But now to our matter.

S. Isidore.

As I haue sayde, through the great report they made of this Vaute, one of the Preests, two of the Schollers and I, tooke with vs a line, & two or three great lights, and so we went to this aforesayde Vaute: we going a long in farder and farder, there we sawe certaine places one aboue an other, three and three on either side, during a great way in length: and these places they sayde, to be some of them the graues of persecuted Saintes and Martires, where they hid them selues in the time of the cruell Emperours of *Roome*, and there they died.

Proceeding on forwarde, we came to an olde thing like an Aultar, wheron, in olde and auncient painting, (which was then almost cleane worne out) was Christ vpon the Crosse, and our Lady and Saint *Iohn* by him: there the Preest sayde, Saint *Peter*, Saint *Paule*, and many other Saintes, had sayde Masse to the Christians that hid them selues there. And besides this (quoth he) there chaunced not many yeeres since, a poore man of the Cittie to come into this Vaute, and when he was come so farre as this Aultar, the light be

THE ENGLISHE

caried in his hand, suddenlie went out, so that he was forced to syt downe, and stay heere.

A straunge and rare miracle, too straunge to be true.

He beeing thus without any light, and ignoraunt of the way to get out againe: fell in prayer to our Lady, who presentlie appeared to him, hauing about her little Angelles, holding burning Lampes in their handes, where through, y[e] place was illumined verie gloriously. / And there she questioned [48 with him, & he with her, about many holy and Religious matters: then she departing, lefte him there accompanied with Angelles, so that he remained there ten dayes, at the ende whereof, he came foorth, and went and tolde the Pope what he had seene, for which, when he died, he was canonized a Saint, and in this order arise many of our Romish Saints.

The Pilgrimage to S. Iames in Gallitia.

As for the Pilgrimage to Saint *Iames* in *Gallitia*, it is a thing that is vsuallie frequented all the yeere, by such a number of people, as you would scantlie iudge: among whome, diuers of our Englishmen be so holie, that they will not stick to beare them company. There they saye, lyeth the bode of Saint *Iames*

Reliques at S. Iames in Gallitia.

the Apostle: and there is the Cocke that crowed, when *Peter* denied Christe: some of the heaire of our Ladies head: certaine of the Thornes of the Crowne of Thorne: the Napkin that was about Christes head in y[e] graue: certayne droppes of his blood: a peece of the Crosse wheron he was crucified, and a number such lyke Reliques, which are honoured and worshipped, as if they were God him selfe.

Then one of the cheefe Pilgrimages, is to a place called *Santa Maria di Loreto*, where, within is an olde little bricke roome, which they name to be the house our Lady dwelt in: there is the Image of our Lady all in Golde and Siluer, the house round about her, beset with Challices of Golde and Siluer, which are oblations and offeringes of diuers Pilgrimes, that come in whole companies thither. And before her is a great barred Chest of iron, wherein they throwe money to our Lady, by whole goblets full at once: Within this little house, there is an Aultar made right before our Lady, & there is sayd euerie day, fortie or fiftie Masses, whereat the people will throng in great heapes, to get into the house, for they thinke them selues happie, if our / Lady [49 haue once seene them. And all the Church is likewise hung with pictures, Tapers, and waxe Candles, which are the vowes of the Pilgrimes to our Lady. I haue heard of some, who by the counsaile of their ghostlie Father, haue made money of all their householde stuffe, and haue come fiue or six hundred mile bare foote and bare legged, to giue it all to our Lady there: meane while, the holy Father hath had

(margin: Pilgrimage to Saint Maria di Loreto.)

(margin: All this helpes to maintaine the Pope.)

libertie, to play with yᵉ mans wife, at &c. In all my life I neuer sawe a place more frequented with people, then this is dayly, onelie for the admirable Miracles yᵗ be done there. Some haue come thither for theyr eye sight: and when they were there, they could see a little (as they say) but they haue come a way stark blind as they were before. A mã came thither, beeing greeuouslie wounded on the Sea, by his enimies: and after he had seene our Lady, he went to the Hospitall, and within a quarter of a yeere after, at the furthest, the Chirurgions had healed him. When he was well againe, he went and hung vp his picture in the Church, that he was healed of his hurt, so soone as he looked vpon our Lady. Diuers haue been brought thither in their Beds, some beeing sick, some wounded, or otherwise diseased: and there they were set before our Lady, looking when she should say: *Take vp thy bed and walke.* And because she could not intend to speake to them, beeing troubled with so many other suters: they haue been caried to the Hospitall, & there they haue been either buried or cured, then such as recouer their health must goe set vp their picture in the Church, howe that the very looking on our Lady hath holpen them. Sũdry other holy Miracles, done by our Lady of *Loreto*, I could rehearse, but they be so

Marginal note: The myracles at our Lady of *Loreto*.

straūge, that no wise body will care for the hearing them: neuerthelesse, the Pope finds her a good sweet Lady of *Loreto*, for ye pilgrimage to her, encreaseth his treasure, many thousãds in a yere. / [50

To *Mount Faulcon*, there is an other Pilgrimage, to see the body of S. *Clare*, which was buried I knowe not howe many hundred yeeres agoe, and yet the body remaineth whole and sound, without any perishing of bone or skin. I haue beene at this place, and there in a long ritch Tabernacle of glasse, lyeth, as they say, the same body of Saint *Clare*: the handes and feete are to be seene, which I can aptlie compare to the manner of the Anotomie, whereon the Chirurgions shewe euerie yeere their cunning, as for any flesh, there is none to be seene: but the bare bones, and the withered sinewes, which beeing kept so brauelie as that is, standing styll in one place and neuer mooued, I iudge will continue a great while, & truelie I take it to be some Anotomie, as diuers other haue done, that haue seene it as well as I. The whole body (if there be any) is couered with a gowne of blacke Veluet, and the head couered, so that none can see it. There lyeth by her, a thing which they say, was her heart, which beeing cleft a sunder in the middest: the whole torment and passion of Christe, was there in

The Pylgrimage to Mount Faulcon, to see Saint Clare

The Reliques of S. Clare.

liuelie forme to be seene. Then there is likewise by her, a glasse of her teares, that she shed daylie, in remembrance of the bitter passion of our Sauiour: which teares, they say, are as fresh and sweet, as they were on the first day.

<small>Other Pilgrimages to diuers places.</small>

There are a number other Pilgrimages, as to *Thurine*, to see the winding sheete wherin Christ was layd: wherein, as they say, he hath left the perfect Image of his body. This meruailous Relique, is neuer showen, but once in foureteen yeere, & then to deceiue the people with the greater aucthority, there must six Cardinalles come thither, and they must holde it abroade for euerie one to see it, no other but they may presume to touch it. To *Paris*, to Saint *Dennis* in *Fraunce*, to *Poiters*, and a nūber other places there be daylie Pilgrimages, to see / a number like Re- [51] liques, as I haue declared before: all these helpe to vpholde the Pope, least his kingdome should decay, and so his vsurping title be cleane worne out of memorie.

<small>A newe Pilgrimage risen vp in *Roome*, called *Madonna di Mōte*.</small>

But now you shall heare of a newe prop and piller, wherewith the Pope is & will be meruailously strengthened, that is risen vp little more then two yeere since: and at this newe holie place, is wrought miracles of great accoumpt. In the yeere of our Lord, 1580. about the time of Easter, a certayne poore man, one that sawe the simplicitie of the people, howe apt they were to beleeue euerie fayned inuention: he beeing a subtile and craftie fellowe, thought he would come in with some deuise of his owne, whereby he might get a great deale of money, & beside, be canonized for a Saint when he dyed.

He hauing concluded his practise, with diuers other craftie companions, as subtile as him selfe, who should maintaine all that he did deuise: fayned him selfe to dreame in his Bed, that a vision appeared to him, wylling him to make cleane his house, and to fall downe and reuerence an olde picture of our Lady, which stoode in his house, when presentlie there should be meruailous miracles accomplished there. His companions noised this abroade, adding thereto such admirable protestation of speeche, as euerie one that heard thereof, conceiued no small cause of wundering. This aforesayd vision appeared to this man twise, all in one manner, by which time it was spread abroade sufficientlie: so that when it came the thirde time, he did according as the voice bade him, he arose, made cleane his house, and fell downe and worshipped the Picture of our Lady.

His companions had some of them, bound vp their legs, & went on Croutches, some of them fayned them / selues to be blinde: so [52

74 *THE ENGLISHE*

<small>Miracles very strãgely wrought.</small>

that they came no sooner before our Lady, but the lame recouered his legges, and the blinde his sight. Then those fewe Croutches, that these counterfeit fellowes came withall, where hung vp by the Picture, and a number more, to make the people beleeue so many lame folkes were healed, and likewise the reporte of the blinde that receiued theyr sight, so that it was thought a meruailous number were healed, at this new found holie place.

<small>Note the meruailovs ignoraunce of these people.</small>

Vpon this, the resort of people thither, was truelie incredible: Gentlemen would come thither, and there hang vp their veluet Cloakes, as an offering to our Lady: Gentlewomen, would come thither bare foote and bare legged, & there hang vp their veluet Gownes, their silke Gownes, with other costlie apparell, and goe home againe in their Peticoates. As for the money, Iuelles, and other treasure daylie offered there, it was most meruailous to see: for therewith they haue builded a verie fayre Church where this house stoode. When they sawe they were growen so ritch, they made no accoumpt of the olde Picture, wherwith all the aforesayd miracles were done: but they erected a costly Aultar, and theron made a sumptuous new Picture of our Lady, which the people doo daylie honour with meruailous resort. This is faithfully affirmed by one *Iohn Young* an Englishe man, who not long since came home from *Roome*, & while he was there, he well noted the impudencie of our English men, in lauding & extolling this place, and the miracles there wrought: so that they as certainlie beleeue in those miracles, as any Christian dooth in God.

This *Iohn Young*, once questioned with one of the English Preestes, why God dyd not as well suffer such miracles to be done by his Son Iesus Christ, as altogether by our Lady: wherto ye Preest aunswered. Because / [53 among the Heretiques, they vse little or no reuerende regard to our Lady, but rather despise & contempne her: therefore it is the will of God, to witnesse the power & heauenlie aucthoritie she hath, by these and many such miracles, bothe heere and in diuers other places, rather then by his sonne Christe. Heere may euerie good Christian, beholde the horrible abuses, vsed among this Sathanicall crew: their Pilgrimages, their Reliques, and all their craftie inuentions, is to be meruailed, that people will be so fonde as to beleeue.

A wise aunswer of an Englishe man.

As for the Nayles wherwith our Sauiour was nailed on the Crosse, it is euidentlie registred by learned writers, that they were no more in number then three: yet I am sure in *Roome*, there is aboue a dozen nayles, dispearsed there through diuers Churches, and

76   *THE ENGLISHE*

they are not ashamed to say, that with euery one of those nailes, Christe was nayled vpon the Crosse.

Helena, the mother of Constātine, the Emperour, found the Crosse of Christe, and gaue the nailes to her sonne.

And for those three Nayles, wherwith Christe was nayled on the Crosse, *Platina* recordeth, that Queene *Helena* the mother of *Constantine* the Emperour, searching in the ground, by chaunce found the Crosse wheron Christ was crucified, & wherin the Nayles were stil sticking, for which cause she builded there a Temple in the same place, where she found the Crosse. All these Nayles she gaue to her sonne *Constantine*, which he bestowed in this order. One of them he caused to be fastened in the bridle of his Horse, whereon he rode to the warres: an other he made to be wrought into his Helmet, in the place where he set his Plume of Feathers: and the third he vsed to carie about with him, tyll on a tyme he sayling on the *Hadriaticum* Sea, a tempest arose, so that the Sea wexed verie rough, wherevpon he cast the Nayle therein, to asswage the rage thereof. Thus haue you heard what became of the three nailes, wherwith our Sauiour was nayled on the Crosse: and / yet it may be, that the Nayle which [54 *Constantine* threw into the Sea (according as *Ambrose* dooth likewise affirme it was) tooke vpon it the nature of a Fishe, and spawned a great many of other Nayles, whereof those

ROMAINE LYFE

may be some, that are helde for such holy Reliques. And because you shall not doubt whether this be the opiniõ of *Platina* or no: I will heere set downe the woords according as they be in his workes. *Platina in vitis Pontificum, et in vita Siluestri primi. Anno. 339. ab vrbe condita. 1191. Helena vero ædificato, eo in loco Templo vbi Crucem repererat, abiens, clauos quibus Christi corpus Cruci affixum fuerat, secum ad filium portat. Horum ille vnum in frœnos Equi transtulit, quibus in prælio vteretur: alio pro cono galiæ vtebatur: tertium in mare Hadriaticum (vt ait Ambrosius) ad compescendas sæuiētis maris procellas deiecit.*

Bishoppe *Iuell*, Bishoppe of *Salisburie*, preaching at *Paules* Crosse, in the beginning of her Maiesties reigne, tooke occasion by his Text, to entreate of a company of the Popishe Reliques, where among he named the Nayles, that nailed Christe on the Crosse, what a company the Papistes had of them: two in one place, two in an other, and heere one, and there an other, so that he could reckon to the number of seuenteen, that they had. And then he tolde, how at a Visitation in his Diocesse, he found a Nayle at a Gentlemans house, which the Gentleman and diuers of his freendes, did worship and reuerence, for one of ye Nayles wherwith Christe was nayled on the Crosse: from him he tooke it, and sayd, I

A Sermon of Bishop Iuell, at Pauls crosse.

haue already reckoned seuenteene in diuers places, and this is the eighteene, which he pulled foorth, and shewed it to all the people. This is the marchandize of *Roome*: from reposing any credite in them, or him that is the Capitoll maister of them, Good Lord deliuer vs. / [55

¶ *The manner of the dissention in the Englishe Colledge, betweene the Englishe men and the VVelsh men: the banishment of the English men out of Roome, and the Popes sending for them againe, with other matters woorthy the reading.*

Chap. 6.

Auing promised before in my Booke, to rehearse after what māner the English men and Welshe men fell at variance in the Colledge: I thought good to driue off the time no further, but euen heere to set downe how and in what sort it was. The Pope when he erected the Colledge, gaue it the name of the Englishe Colledge, so that he supposed the Welshe and Englishe, to be all as one, in that they came all out of one Countrey, allowing them his liberalitie ioyntlie togeather. Now in deede there are sundrie Welsh Doctors in *Roome*, who haue been longest, & of greatest familiaritie with the Cardinall *Morone*, who was the Protector of the English Colledge, to whome likewise he allowed greatest fauour, so that imboldening them selues vppon him, the Welsh men would be Lordes ouer the English men, and vse them according as they thought good.

Doctor *Morris*, beeing a Welsh man, and *Custos* of the Hospitall or Colledge, would allowe his owne Coūtreimen greater preheminence then English men: / which indeede [56 they began to stomack, and would not esteme him for their gouernour, but rather sought to haue the *Iesuites* to rule them, by whom they applied their studies, and beside, they woulde bee indifferent men on eyther parte.

Doctour Morris, fauoured more his owne Countreymen then English men.

When I had beene there a pretty while, I know not how Doctor *Morris* conceiued anger against me, but he would not suffer me to tarry any longer in ye Colledge. As for my fellow, his sinceritye in their religion was such, his naturall disposition so agreeable with theirs, and euery thing hee did esteemed so well: that Doctor *Morris* would suffer him willingly to remain there, but he could not abide me in any case. The Schollers vnderstanding this, as well they that bare me affection, as they that made least account of me, agreed to take my parte, saying. That if Doctor *Morris* would put euery Englishman, he thought good on, out, in short time the Colledge would be all Welsh men: so they bad me stick to them, and if I went away, they would goe away too.

The English mens policee to keepe me there still.

Beside, they mooued a certaine speech amongst themselues, that if I were not receiued into the Colledge amongst them, and vsed in euery respect according as they were: when I returned into Englande, being knowen to come from *Roome*, I might be compelled to tell the names of them that were there, and what conference I had among them, so that their parentes and freendes shoulde be discouered, and them selues be knowen against their comming into England. To auoyde therefore any such doubt, vntill they had mee sworne to Preesthood: they would keepe me there, and then I should be as deepe in any matter as they.

When I perceiued ye scope of their deuise, I behaued my selfe more frowardly to Doctor *Morris*, thẽ euer I did before: euery thing y^t I hearde of him, I tolde vnto ye Schollers, and taried there dinner & supper in spight of his nose. Where vpon he went and complayned

to / the Cardinall *Morone*, howe the [57
Schollers vsed no regarde to him, being their
Rector, but maintained one lately come foorth
of England, both to scorn at him, and to offer
him too much abuse.

This beeing come to the Schollers eare, and
howe on the nexte daye they muste appeare
before the Cardinall: they determined with
themselues all one resolute opinion, which
was, that Doctor *Morris* shoulde bee Rector
ouer them no longer, but the *Iesuites* that were
kept in the house for the profite of theyre
studies, and vppon this they woulde all stande,
denyinge anye Rectorshippe to Doctor *Morris*.

On the morrowe they were sent for before
the Cardinall *Morone*, where they founde
Doctor *Morris*, and Doctor *Lewes*, they
hauing made sounde theyre tale before they
came. When they were come into the
presence of the Cardinall and my selfe with
them, these, or the verye like speeches hee
vsed vnto vs in Latine.

The Schollers were sent for before the Cardinal, vpon the complaint of Doctor Morris.

You Englishmen, what meaneth this great
disobedience, and vnciuil behauioure you vse
in your Colledge? Maister Doctor *Morris*, a
man of auncient time, and well estemed heere
in the Cittie, being appoynted to bee your
Rector, and to gouerne you in a good order,
as a greate while hee hath done: you contrarye
to looue and duetye, behaue your selues

ridiculouslye againste him, and neyther respecting his credite and countenaunce, nor your owne honestye, determine a mutenie or tumulte amonge your selues. What is the cause of this? you are sent for to manifeste it, wherefore lette mee heare howe you can excuse thys blame layde agaynste you.

Maister *Sherwin*, who was executed with *Campion*, beeing there esteemed a singuler Scholler, bothe for / his eloquence, as also [58 his learning: made aunswer for them all after this manner.

<small>Mayster *Sherwins* aunswer to the Cardinal, on the behalfe of them all.</small>

I truste my gratious Lorde, by that time you haue hearde, the good cause we haue to stirre in this matter: you will neyther bee offended at our proceeding, nor displeased with vs, the cause tending to your owne honoure. It is not vnknowen to you, that the Colledge or Hospitall, which by the gratious prouidence of our deere Father the Popes holinesse, wee enioye our abydinge in at thys presente: hath beene alwayes allowed suche a sufficient stipende, that one shoulde not bee better then an other, or excell his fellowe in common behauiour.

This moste godlye and holye appointed estate: we both haue beene, and at this present are, content to obeye: but when hee that is the heade shall fayle in hys dutye, and vrge an inconuenience among a quiet assemblie: no meruayle if the Woorme turne, beeing troden vppon, and wee speake, beeing vsed with too much spyght.

Maister Doctor *Morris*, whose age wee reuerence, and obeye the title of hys authoritye: dealing with vs so vnfreendlye as hee dooth, we can hardlye beare it, muche lesse abyde it. For where his office dooth commaunde him to deale bothe iuste and vprightlye, and to vse no partialitye to eyther, for fauoure or alliaunce: he dooth not onelye abuse the credite of hys authorytye, but also maliciouslye deale with vs, who haue not so much as vsed an euil thought against him.

When any Englishman commeth to the Hospitall if hys learning bee neuer so good, or hys behauioure neuer so decent: excepte hee bee pleased, hee shall not be enterteyned. But if a Welshman come, yf hee bee neuer so vylde a Runnagate, neuer so / lewde a [59 person, he can not come so soone as he shall bee welcome to him, whither he haue any learning or no, it maketh no matter, he is a Welshman, and hee must be permitted. Then which of vs hath the beste gowne, he must receiue one that is all ragged and torne, and the newcome Welshman must haue the best, because he is the *Custos* Countreiman: and many nightes hee must haue the Welshmen in his chamber, where they must be merry at

Doctor *Morris*, kinde to his owne Coũteremen.

84   THE ENGLISHE

theyr good cheere, we glad to sitte in our
studies, and haue an ill supper, because M.
Doctor wasteth our Commons vpon his owne
Countrymen, so that we must be content with
a snatch and away.

If there be one bed better then an other, the
Welshman must haue it, if there be any
Chamber more hansome then an other, the
Welshman must lodge there: in breefe, the
thinges of moste account are the Welshmens
at commaund.

This maketh many of vs to wish our selues
Welsh men, because we woulde gladly haue
so good prouision as they, & being Countrymen to our *Custos*, we should be all vsed alike:
excepting Maister Doctors Nephew *Mor-
ganus Clenokus*, he must be in his silke,
though all the rest goe in a sacke.

They desire the Iesuits for their gouernours.

To mittigate therefore all inconueniences,
that neither the Englishmen shall be de-
spised, nor the Welshmen contemned: we
desire that the *Iesuites* in our Colledge, may
receiue the Rectorship, they labour for the
profit of our studies, and they being none of
our nation or country, will see equity vsed to
eyther side: so, our discorde shall be quietly
reformed, our Colledge a great deale better
gouerned, our selues be encouraged to im-
ploye vs more willingly to our studies, and
wee shall ioyntly liue together in quietnes.

Where other wise, our emulation shall be knowen at home in our Country, how we fall at variaunce heere, and can not agree: and then shall our names bee knowen, our parentes / and freendes openly discouered, [60 then what the end will be, I leaue to your honorable iudgement.

When the Cardinall had heard this discourse, (beeing greatly affected to Doctor *Morris*, thorow his long abiding in *Roome*) he would not graunt that he should be put from his office, but bad thẽ depart home again, and shew themselues obedient to the Rector, that both the Pope and him selfe had appointed, promising if hee heard any more disturbaunce, hee would informe the Pope of it, which should bee but small to their profite.

[Side note: The Cardinall so affected Doctor Morris, that he shoulde not leaue his Rectorshippe.]

So the Cardinall not minded to heare them any longer at that time, they departed home to the Colledge, greatly offended with them selues that they had spedde no better. And now, I must out of the Colledge there was no other remedy: but yet thorowe entreaty of the *Iesuites*, I had leaue for a fortnight to lye in a verye sweete Chamber, filled with old rusty Iron, and all the trash of the house was put into that Chamber, beeing a vacãt place, & seruing for no other purpose, because it was next to the cõmon house of office, which ayred the Chamber with so sweete a perfume:

that but for names sake of a Chamber, and
feare of catching some disease, I had rather
haue lyen in the streete amongst the Beggers.
Well, froward as I was, so was I frowardlye
serued, which I thinke Doctor *Morris* did,
onely to tame my youthfulnesse: for in this
place, not long before my comming to *Roome*,
there lay one tormented with a Deuill, and so
distraught of hys wits, that they were fayne to
binde him there in his bed.

Doctor *Morris* his prouision for my lodging.

So Doctor *Morris*, seeing I vsed my selfe,
both carelesse of him, and with little regarde
to theyr Religion, yet in such an order as they
coulde haue small aduauntage of me: cham-
bred me there, where I thinke the Deuill was
still left, for euery night there was such a
coyle among the old Iron, such ratling and
throwing downe the Boordes, that with the
sweete smell came / out of the counting [61
house to my Beddes heade: I lay almost feared
out of my wits, and almost choked with that
pleasaunt perfume, so that when I was layd in
my Bed, I durst not stirre till it was fayre
broad day, that I might perceiue euerye
corner of my Chamber, whither the Deuill
were there or no.

Euery morning the Priests & the Schollers
woulde come to visite me, giuing me money
to send for my dinner and supper into the
Towne: because Doctor *Morris* myne olde

freende, watched them so neere, that I could not haue so muche as a draughte of Wine in the house. Then I tolde them of the noyse that was euery night in my Chamber, when they verily beleeued, that the Deuill, hauing possessed a Woman on the furder side of the Garden: dyd euery night take vp his lodgeing in my Chamber among the olde Iron.

Wherefore one night, two of the Priestes came to hallow my Chamber, and broughte their holy water, and their holy Candles, and sprinckled about in euery corner: giuing me also a pot of holy water, to hang by my Beds side, that when I heard the sturre agayne, I should with the sprinckling Brush, throw it about the Chamber. And they gaue me a payre of Beads, wheron I should say sixe *Pater nosters*, and sixe *Aue Mariaes*, then they would warraunt me, the noyse would be gon strayght way.

<small>The preests come with holy water to hallowe my Chamber.</small>

Night came, and supping so well as I coulde, with two *Quatrines* woorth of Leekes, one *Quatrine* bestowed in *Ricoct*, which is harde Cruds to make Cheese, a *Bayock* in bread, and a *demie Boccale*, of the *Vine Romanesco*, wherewith I supped so wel as I might, albeit not so well as I would, yet a little thing serues to quench hunger. I had not beene in my Bedde full an hower and an halfe, not daring to sleepe for feare, nor keepe my

<small>The manner of my supper at night.</small>

head out of the Bed, because of myne accustomed ayre; but then began the noyse againe, more vehe- / ment then the night [62 before, the olde Iron was flung about the Chamber, the Boordes that leaned against the Wall fell downe, and such a terrible coyle there was, that I thoughte the house woulde haue fallen on my head.

Then I put foorth my hand to throw the holy water about, which did as much good, as the thing is good of it selfe: which set me in such a chafe, that to make vp the Musique among the olde Iron, I sent the potte and the holy water, with as much force as I could. As for my Beades, I was so impatient with my selfe, that I gaue them the place which they best deserued: and then I called to old Sir *Robert* a Welsh Priest, who lay in a pretty Chamber hard by, but before he woulde come, the noyse was indifferently pacified. For hee comming with a Candle in his hãd, which he vsed to keepe alight in his Chamber, and beeing in haste, fell ouer a stone thresholde that laye in hys way: so that he burste hys knee verye sore, and coulde not lighte his Candle againe in the space of an hower, by whych time all was quiet.

<small>S. *Robert* a Welsh Prieste, comming to see what was the cause of the noyse, fell ouer a thresholde and break hys knee.</small>

The feare I tooke at thys noyse, brought me to bee very weake and sickly, so that I was very vnwillinge to lye there any longer. But

Doctor *Morris* I thanke him was so gentle to me, that he sayde, and if I lyked not my lodgeing, goe hardly (quoth hee) and lye in the streete, for that place is more meete for thee then any roome in the house.

Howe I receyued these churlishe woordes, I leaue to your iudgementes, but it suffyseth, I gaue hym my blessynge, and yf I coulde haue gotten hym foorth of *Roome*, I woulde haue bumd hym too.

On the nexte daye, vppon an other complaynte of Doctor *Morris*, the Students were all sent for again before the Cardinall: who playnly sayd vnto them, that / except they [63 would liue in quietnes one with an other, (because there was one *Hugh Griffin*, a Welshman of a hote nature, and he would many times fall together by the eares with some of the Schollers, that somtime the blood ran about theyr eares) likewise, y^t they should confesse Doctor *Morris* for theyr rightfull Rector, and be obedient to what he appoynted: or els to get them away out of *Roome*.

Well home they came againe, incensed with such anger and choller, that they were nowe more disobedient then before: saying to Doctor *Morris*, that they would neuer consent vnto him, and therefore prouided them selues to be packing out of *Roome*. Doctor *Morris* thinking to bring them violently to his bowe, informed the Cardinall so seuerely against them: that they were sent for the third time, when he commaunded thē to prouide themselues, for they should stay no longer in the English Hospitall, but banished them all from the Cittie.

<small>Doctor *Morris* beginneth to offer me gentlenes.</small>

When they were come to the Colledge, euery man trussed vp his needefull thinges, determining on the next morning to departe: then came Doctor *Morris* to me and my fellow, willing vs to stay, because the other would be gon, and he would stand our freend meruailously. Trust me no Sir (quoth I) since you would not stand my freende when I was in great neede, now I meane not to receiue your courtesie when I care not for it: for since the Students haue stoode my freendes so much, and you mine enemy so greatly, I will beare a share in their trauaile how euer I speede. As for my fellow, since you haue looued him all this while, looue him now too if you please: and let him stay & doo what you thinke best, for I haue tolde you my minde.

<small>The Englishmen auoide the Colledge.</small>

Well, on the morrow morning wee went our way, with bag and baggage, to an Englishmans house in the Cittie, and as I remember, his name was M. *Creede*, / [64 where to make ready our dinner, euerie one tooke an office vpon him, one to fetch milke, an other to make ready Rice for

ROMAINE LYFE

the pottage, some to make the fire: so that euerie one was imployed till our dinner was dispatched. Then they concluded to buie euerie man an Asse, to carrie his Bookes and his cloathes vpon, as for money, there were Gentlemens sonnes of such credite amongst them, that Doctor *Moorton*, and the Gentlemen in the Cittie, would prouide them with as good as fiue hundred Crownes quicklie. Within one hower and a halfe after dinner, came Father *Alfonso* the *Iesuit* of the English Colledge, whome the Students had chosen, and made sute to be their Rector: he, I say, came running in such haste, that he could hardly tell his tale, because he was almost out of breath. But this was the summe of his newes, that the Popes holinesse had sent for them in all the haste, and they must delay no time, but come to him with all speede possible.

The Schollers sent for before the Pope.

Then we went with him to the Popes Pallace, where comming into the Popes Chamber, and hauing euerie one kissed his foote: we stayde to attende what was his pleasure. But before he spake any woorde, with a dissembling and hippocriticall countenaunce, he fell into teares, which trickled downe his white beard: and began in Latin with these, or the very like woords. O you English men, to whome my looue is such, as I

H

can no way vtter, considering that for me you haue left your Prince, which was your duetie, and come so farre to me, which is more then I can deserue: yet as I am your refuge, when persecution dealeth straightly with you in your Countrey, by reason of the hereticall Religion there vsed, so will I be your Bulwarke to defend you, your guide to protect you, your Father to nourish you, and your freend with my hart blood to doo you any profite. / [65

Beholde, what deceites the deuill hath to accomplish his desire? teares, smoothe speeches, liberallitie, and a thousand meanes: to make a man carelesse of God, disobedient to his Prince, and more, to violate vtterlie the faith of a Subiect. These teares that he shed, these woordes that he spake, made diuers of them say within them selues, as one of them for example, presentlie to me sayde.

The words of one of the Schollers.

Oh singuler Saint, whose life, looue, and liberalitie, may be a spectacle to the whole world. Who would liue in *England*, vnder the gouernment of so vile a *Iezabell*: and may rest in safetie vnder the perfect Image of Iesus? who would not forsake Father, Mother, freends, goods, yea, and the life it selfe: to haue the bountifull blessing of such a prouident Father? The Pope recouering his health againe from his weeping: caused this deuout fellowe to stay his talke, because he began againe as thus.

What is the cause that you will depart from me, that haue so well prouided for you: to thrust your selues on the rocke of your owne destruction? Then Maister *Sherwin* began, and tolde him all the dealinges of Doctor *Morris* towarde them, according as he had done before to the Cardinall, and how they would haue the *Iesuites* for their Gouernours, for the causes before mentioned. Vpon these woordes the Pope started out of his Chayre. Why (quoth he) I made the Hospitall for Englishe men, and for their sake I haue giuen so large exhibition: and not for the Welsh men. Returne to your Colledge againe, you shall haue what you will desire, and any thing I haue in the worlde to doo you good.

The Pope supposed Englishmē and Welshe men, all as one.

Then he commaunded one of the cheefe Gentlemen of his Chamber, to goe with vs, and to certifie the Popes minde to Doctor *Morris*, and so giuing vs his / benediction, [66 we all went merilie againe to the Colledge.

The Gentleman gaue Doctour *Morris* to vnderstande, he must be Rector no longer, the *Iesuite* named Father *Alfonso*, whom the Schollers had chosen, must haue his office, then were the Schollers glad, that they had gotten the victorie of the Welshmen.

On the morrowe, the Pope sent fowre

The Popes ly-berallite.

hundred Crownes, to newe reparation the house, to buie the Students all needefull thinges that they wanted, and the house must no longer be called a Colledge, but a Seminarie.

Then Cardinall *Morone*, because Doctor *Morris* should not loose all his dignitie, caused the house to be parted, and so made bothe a Seminarie for the Studientes, and an Hospitall for the entertainement of Englishe Pilgrimes when they came, whereof Doctor *Morris* continued *Custos*, by the Popes appointment.

Thus was the strife ended, and my selfe and my fellowe, admitted by the Popes owne consent, to be Schollers there: but yet the sicknesse I gotte, with lying in my former Chamber, hung styll vppon mee, so that I was then remooued to a verie fayre Chamber, where the Schollers euery daye would come and visite me, vntyll such tyme as I recouered my health againe. /

[67

¶ *Of the* Carne vale *in* Roome: *the Popes generall curssing on* Maunde Thursdaie: *and the manner of the* Flagellante *that night.*

Chap. 7.

Vring the time of Shreuetide, there is in *Roome* kept a verie great coyle, which they vse to call the *Carne vale*, which endureth the space of three or fowre dayes, all which time, the Pope keepeth him selfe out of *Roome*, so great is the noyse and hurlie burlie. The Gentlemen will attire them selues in diuers formes of apparell, some lyke Women, other lyke Turkes, and euerie one almost in a contrarie order of disguising: and eyther they be on Horsebacke, or in Coatches, none of them on foote, for the people that stand on the grounde to see this pastime, are in verie great daunger of their liues, by reason of the running of Coatches and great Horses, as neuer in all my life did I see the lyke sturre. And all this is done where the *Courtezanes* be, to shew them delight and pastime, for they haue Couerlettes layde out at their windowes, whereon they stand leaning

The *Burdella*, helpes to maintaine the Pope.

foorth, to receiue diuers deuises of Rose water, and sweete odours in their faces, which the Gentlemen will throwe vp to their windowes.

During this time, euery one weareth a disguised visor on his face, so that no one knowes what or whẽce they / be: and if any one beare [68 a secrete mallice to an other, he may then kill him, & no body will lay hands on him, for all this time they will obey no lawe. I sawe a braue *Romaine*, who rode there verie pleasant in his Coatch, and suddenlie came one, who discharged a Pistoll vpon him, yet no body made any accoumpt, eyther of the murderer, or the slaine Gentleman: beside, there were diuers slaine, bothe by villanie, and the Horsses or the Coatches, yet they continued on their pastime, not making any regard of them.

The first daye of their *Carne vale*, the Iewes in *Roome* cause an Ensigne to be placed at the Capitoll, where likewise they appoint certaine wagers at their owne coastes: and then they runne starke naked from *Porta populo* vnto the Capitoll for them, the which I iudge aboue a myle in length. And all the way, they gallop their great Horsses after them, and carie goades with sharpe pointes of steele in them: wherewith they will pricke the Iewes on the naked skin, if so be they doo not runne faster then their Horsses gallop, so that you shall see some of their backs all on gore

[marginal note:] The Iewes haue small pastime in this. But it is an order that they must doo, whether they wyll or no.

blood. Then he that is foremost, and soonest commeth to the Capitoll, he is set on a Horse backe without any saddle, one going before him carying the Ensigne: but then you shall see a hundred boyes, who haue prouided a number of Orrenges, they will so pelt the poore Iewe, that before he can get vp to the Capitoll, he will be beaten beside his Horse fowre or fiue times.

The next day, there are certaine of the Christians that runne naked likewise, but no body pursueth them, either with Horse or Coatch: and the wager they run for, the Iewes must pay likewise. Then the Buffell and the Asse runneth, but it is vnpossible for me to tell all the knauerie vsed about this: and therefore thus much shall suffise of the *Carne vale*, letting you vnder-/stand, that they who were most [69 knauishlie disposed in this sporte, on *Ashwednesday* came to take Ashes in such meeke order, as though it had neuer beene they.

ON *Maunde Thursday*, the Pope commeth into his Gallerie ouer Saint *Peters*, sitting in the Chayre wherwith he is caried on mennes shoulders: and there he hath a great painted holie Candle in his hande burning, when as a Cardinall on eche side of him, the one in Latin, the other in Italian, sĩgeth the Popes generall malediction.

98   THE ENGLISHE

<small>The Popes cursses will returne to him selfe.</small>

There he cursseth the Turke, and her Maiestie, our most gratious Princesse and Gouernesse, affirming her to be farre wurse then the Turke, or the cruellest Tiraunt that is. He cursseth likewise all *Caluinians*, *Lutherans*, *Zwinglians*, and all that are not according to his disposition. When he hath curssed all that he can, saying, *Amen*, he letteth the Candle fall: when as the people will skamble for it, and euerie one catch a lyttle peece if they can, yea, our English men will be as busie as the best, and one of them chaunced to gette a peece of the waxe of the Candle, whereof he made such a bragging

<small>VVas this the part of a Subiect?</small>

when he came to the Colledge, as you will not thinke, that he had got a peece of the Candle, wherwith the Queene of *England* was curssed, and that he would keepe it so long as he liued.

<small>The manner of the *Flagellāte*.</small>

The same night a number of the basest people, and most wicked liuers that be amongst the people, gather them selues togeather in companies: as the company of the *Holie Ghost*, the companie of *Charitie*, the cõpany of *Death*, and such like, euerie company their *Crucifix* before them, their singers following them, on eyther side a number of burning Torches, and thus they goe all whipping them selues.

First they go vp into the Popes Pallace, & then down / into Saint *Peters* Church, which [70 is all adorned with a number of waxe lyghtes: and there on the toppe of an Aultar standeth a couple of Cardinalles, who sheweth them the holie Handkercher, or *Vultus sanctus*, (which in deede is nothing but a liuelie painted Picture, ouershaddowed with a couple of fine Lawnes, and no body must desire to see it vncouered, because they say no body is able to endure the brightnesse of the face, a number haue seene it, and haue beene the wurse a great whyle after) and all the while that bothe this, and the Speare head is showne, they will whippe them selues before them verie greeuouslie, and giue a generall clamor thorowe the Church: *Misericordia, Misericordia, Tu autem Domine miserere nobis:* and in this order they continue almoste the whole night. This is the glorie of the Pope, the blindnesse of the people, and the great follie of our English men, to bring them selues within the compasse of such wicked order of lyfe.

A fine peece of knauerie, to deceyue the people.

God continue his loouing and fatherlie countenaunce ouer *Englande*: blesse and preserue her Maiestie, and her Honourable Councell: and exercise vs all in feare to him, obedience to her, and faithfull and continuall looue to our neighbours. *Amen.* /

THE ENGLISHE

❧ *A true Report, of the Christian suffering, and mercilesse martirdome, of one* Richard Atkins, *English man, at* Roome: *who for the trueth of the Gospel, to the great terrour of all the beholders, endured the extremitie of the torment, and cruell agonie of death, in the yeere of our Lord.* 1581.

Chap. 8.

About the time of Midsommer, in the yeere. 1581. one *Richard Atkins*, a *Hartfoord* shyre man, came to *Roome*, and hauing found the Englishe Colledge, he knocked at the doore, when as diuers of the Studentes came to welcome him, knowing that he was an Englishe man. Among other talke, they willed him to goe the Hospitall, and there to receiue his meate and lodging, according as the order was appointed, whereto he aunswered. I come not (my Countreymen) to any such intent as you iudge, but I come loouinglie, to rebuke the great misorder of your liues, which I greeue to heare, and pittie to beholde. I come likewise to let your prowde Antechrist vnder-

<small>His councell to his Countreymen.</small>

ROMAINE LYFE 101

stand, that he dooth offend the heauenlie Maiestie, rob God of his honour, and poysoneth the whole world with his abhominable blasphemies: making them homage Stocks and Stones, and that filthy Sacrament, which is nothing else but a foolish Idoll.

When they heard these woordes, one *Hugh Griffin*, a / Welshe man, and a Student in [72 the Colledge, caused him to be put in the Inquisition: where, howe they examined him, and how he aunswered them, I know not, but after certayne dayes he was set at lybertie againe.

And one day going in the streete, he met a Preest carying the Sacrament, which offending his cōscience, to see the people so croutch and kneele to it: he caught at it to haue throwne it downe, that all the people might see what they worshipped. But missing his purpose, and beeing iudged by the people, that he did catch at the holinesse, that (they say) commeth from the Sacrament, vppon meere deuotion: he was let passe, and nothing sayde to him.

1. His attempt, to smite downe the Sacrament.

Fewe dayes after, he came to Saint *Peters* Church, where diuers Gentlemen & other, were hearing Masse, and the Preest beeing at the eleuation: he vsing no reuerence, stepped amongst the people to the Aultar, and threwe downe the Challice with the Wine, striuing

2. His attempte in S. *Peters* Church.

likewise to haue pulled the Cake out of the Preestes handes. For which, diuers rose vp, and beate him with their fystes, and one drew his Rapier, and would haue slaine him: so that in breefe, he was caried to prison, where he was examined, wherefore he committed such an hainous offence: whereto he aunswered, that he came purposelie for that intent, to rebuke the Popes wickednesse, and their Idolatrie. Vpon this, he was condempned to be burned: which sentence he sayde, he was right willing to suffer, and the rather, because the summe of his offence, pertayned to the glorie of God.

<small>Our English mennes labouring to him, and his perswading them.</small>

During the time he remained in prison, sundry English men came vnto him, willing him to be sory for that he had done, and to recant from his dampnable opiniõ: but all the meanes they vsed were in vaine, he confuted their dealinges by diuers places of Scripture. & willed them to be sorie for their wickednesse, while God dyd / permit them time, [73 else they were in daunger of euerlasting dampnation: these woordes made the Englishe men depart, for they could not abide to heare them.

<small>3. His going to execution.</small>

Within a while after, he was set vpon an Asse, without any saddle, he beeing from y̶ᵉ middle vpward naked, hauing some English Preestes with him, who talked to him, but he regarded them not, but spake to ye people in so good language as he could, and tolde them they were in a wrong way, and therfore willed them for Christes cause, to haue regard to the sauing of their soules.

All the way as he went, there were fowre did nothing else, but thrust at his naked body with burning Torches: whereat he neither mooued nor shrunke one iote, but with a cheerefull countenaunce, laboured styll to perswade the people, often bending his body to meete the Torches as they were thrust at him, & would take them in his owne hand, and holde them burning styll vppon his body, whereat the people not a little wundered. Thus he continued almost the space of halfe a mile, tyl he came before Saint *Peters*, where the place of Execution was. When he was come to the place of Execution, there they had made a deuise, not to make the fire about him, but to burne his legges first, which they did, he not dismaying any whit, but suffered all meruailous cheerefully, which mooued the people to such a quandarie, as was not in *Roome* many a day. Then they offered him a Crosse, and willed him to imbrace it, in token that he dyed a Christian: but he put it away with his hand, telling them, that they were euill men to trouble him with such paltrie, when he was preparing him selfe to God,

Oh meruailous patience, and Christian boldnesse.

4.

They offerd him a Cros to imbrace.

whome he behelde in Maiestie and Mercie, ready to receaue him into the eternal rest. They seeing him styll in that minde, departed, saying: Let vs goe, and leaue him to the deuill, whome he serues. Thus ended this faithfull Soldier and Mar- / tir of Christe: [74 who is no doubt in glorie with his Maister, whereto God graunt vs all to come. *Amen*.

THis is faithfullie auouched by the aforesayde *Iohn Young*, who was at that time, and a good while after in *Roome*, in seruice with Maister Doctor *Moorton*: who seeing the Martirdome of this man, when he came home to his house, in the presence of Maister *Smithson*, Maister *Creed*, and the sayd *Iohn Young* his seruaunt, spake as followeth. Surely, this fellow was meruailous obstinate, he nothing regarded the good councell was vsed to him, nor neuer shrunke all the way, when the Torches were thrust at his naked body. Beside, at the place of Execution, he did not faint or crie one iote in the fire, albeit they tormented him verie cruelly, and burned him by degrees, as his legges first, to put him to the greater pain, yet all this he did but smile at. Doubtlesse, but that the woord of God can be but true, else we might iudge this fellowe to be of God: for who could haue suffered so much paine as he did? but truely I beleeue the deuill was in him.

Beholde (good Reader) how they doubt among them selues, and because they will not speake against their Maister the Pope, they inferre ye mighty power of God, vpon the deuill: but he no doubt one day will scatter the chaffe, & gather his chosen Corne into his Garner. That we may be of this good Corne, let vs defie the Pope, his hellish abhominations, continue in our duetie to God, faithfull obedience to her Maiestie, and unity among vs all as Brethren: and then no doubt but we shall enter the land of the liuing, to our eternall . comfort and consolation.

FINIS. *Anthonie Munday*.

The Picture heerin adioyned, dooth liuely decipher the order of the Martirdom, of the aforesaid *Richard Atkins*, at *Roome*. /

ERRATA

The following emendations only have been made in the text of the original:—

Page	Line		In the Original reads:
17	4	'booke hath'	'bookehath'
19	15	'asked'	'as ked'
56	15	'Englishmen'	'Eng- men'
71 72	5 19		The numbering of pp. 50 and 51 is transposed in the original
79	30	'remain there'	'remainthere'
88	sidenote 'break'		'berak'
90	27	M. *Creede* /	'M. *Creede* / *Creed*'
97	29	'sīgeth'	'sigeth'